Everyday Law for Everyone

John C. Howell

LIBERTY HOUSE

FIRST EDITION
SECOND PRINTING

Copyright © 1987 by John Cotton Howell
Printed in the United States of America

Library of Congress Cataloging in Publication Data

Howell, John Cotton, 1926-
    Everyday law for everyone / by John C. Howell.
       p. cm.
    Includes index.
    ISBN 0-8306-3011-2 (pbk.)
    1. Law—United States—Popular works.   I. Title.
KF387.H6331987
349.73—dc19
[347.3]   87-16108
                                           CIP

TAB BOOKS Inc. offers software for
sale. For information and a catalog,
please contact TAB Software Department,
Blue Ridge Summit, PA 17294-0850.

Questions regarding the content of this book
should be addressed to:

    Reader Inquiry Branch
    Editorial Department
    TAB BOOKS Inc.
    Blue Ridge Summit, PA 17294-0214

Everyday Law for Everyone

Contents

Introduction

Most Americans are generally intimidated by the law and lawyers. However, neither law nor lawyers should be thought of as so imposing, majestic, or enigmatic. Although it is true that lawyers have a reputation for complicating the most commonplace issues and many laws are quite incomprehensible to most of us, the term *law* can be defined as the set of rules by which we govern ourselves, and lawyers are merely our employees.

Of course, this is a simplistic overstatement of the point that we elect our lawmakers and are responsible for their acts. "We The People" established our form of government about 200 years ago by adopting the U.S. Constitution and the Bill of Rights as the foundation of a truly democratic society. Whatever resistence you might have to your participation in this concept, it is true that we, as voters, are responsible for the laws and we elect the lawmakers. Thus, under our system of government, the law is composed of that body of rules we establish to govern ourselves, and not, as Sir William Blackstone said, "A rule of civil conduct prescribed by the supreme power of a state, commanding what is right and prohibiting what is wrong," a definition that was accurate in Blackstone's time.

Although we might not wish to take too much direct responsibility for the activities of our elected officials, we do have another choice: we can learn more about our laws, learn more about the people who administer them, and learn more about lawyers. We can change the laws; we can elect new people to enact and administer them.

This guide will give you an introduction to the law, to those rules with which you are most likely to be confronted in your daily activities. It can help you handle many of the family law problems that swirl around you from time to time, such as wills, divorces, avoiding probate, change of name, and others. Business law topics are discussed, and you can follow step-by-step directions to form your own corporation, prepare partnership agreements, prepare business contracts, win landlord-tenant disputes, or stay out of jail.

The fascinating story about the development of law will captivate you, excite the history "buff" in you, and might well motivate you to look further into the writings of Hammurabi, Justinian, Marcus Aurelius, Alexander the Great, and others who shaped and fashioned the course of law and history.

Learning about the development of law is not only satisfying to the mind. It is entertaining and can be most rewarding for those who want to know why human beings, as individuals and as societies, do the things they do, and why there are so many laws that are designed to control so many activities and subjects.

You will learn how to handle many legal problems yourself, and you can learn enough about any specific legal issue to put yourself in a controlling position when you hire a lawyer to represent you in any particular case. You will be able to accomplish all of your objectives when you effectively communicate with lawyers, rather than being intimidated by them.

This guide will help you with legal matters that you can handle yourself, and help you communicate with your lawyer effectively in those cases where you need a lawyer. *Note:* Because statutes and court decisions vary by states and are subject to modifications, no liability is assumed by the author or publisher regarding the use of this book.

(*Editor's Note:* The citations listed in the footnotes throughout this book are the correct legal citations. Your law librarian will be able to assist you in locating the correct reference book.)

Chapter 1

The Self-Help Concept

Shakespeare might not have wanted to "kill all the lawyers," but his often-quoted phrase did reflect the attitude of his times. Samuel Johnson might have been jesting when he said, "I do not wish to speak ill of any man behind his back, but the fact is that he is an attorney." Voltaire reflected the attitude of all times when he said, "Only twice in my life have I felt utterly ruined: once when I lost a lawsuit and once when I won."

Lawyers always have had supreme difficulties in achieving the lofty respectability they claim for themselves. The American colonists brought with them a traditional distrust of lawyers. Several colonies prohibited pleading for hire in the seventeenth century. This prejudice and distrust of lawyers became an institution in America, and it lives on today.

A former chief justice of the United States only a few years ago referred to lawyers as "a sick profession" marked by "incompetence, lack of training, misconduct and bad manners." He concluded that "Ineptness, bungling, malpractice, and bad ethics can be observed in court houses all over this country every day." His assertion that a large percentage of the lawyers who appear in court are incompetent has not been dispelled by recent events.

A Harvard law professor said the legal system in this country is an "expensive, inefficient, frequently incomprehensible nonsystem that often seems contrived to serve lawyers rather than law." In a recent *American Bar Association* report, it was disclosed that two out of three people who need legal help do not get it. According to a *Consumer Reports* survey, 68 percent of the people questioned did not consult lawyers because they believed, "most lawyers charge more for their services than they are worth."

According to a report of an assembly sponsored by the American Bar Association:

> The bar should encourage the trend toward various devices permitting settlement of estates with little or no court involvement of lawyers. The development of procedures for transferring property without administration should be encouraged, as should 'do-it-yourself techniques.'[1]

An article entitled "Do It Yourself: ABA Backs Self-Help Study," states:

> . . . the challenge for the organized bar is to educate the public about when a lawyer may or may not be necessary . . .[2]

John Naisbitt, author of the best-selling book *Megatrends* said:

> Just as we have begun to look after our own health with diet, nutrition, exercise and home test kits for blood pressure or pregnancy, so too will we be more inclined to do our own simple legal procedures — wills, name changes, adoptions and even divorces and bankruptcies — often assisted by a clerk or self-help manual. This trend is reinforced when seen as a way to cut costs as well.[3]

This recitation of perjorative comments about lawyers and the efforts of the public to avoid them is not meant to denigrate all lawyers. The mere fact that some lawyers are dishonest or incompetent does not mean this cognomen should apply to all of them. To the general public, however, it is somewhat like saying that all pit bulls don't bite and that all rattlesnakes don't

---

[1] *American Bar Association Journal,* January 1977:688.
[2] Ibid. April 1983:433.
[3] "Megatrends for Layers and Clients," Ibid., June 1984:45.

strike. Our society has a deep distrust of lawyers that simply will not go away.

Notwithstanding this indescribably untidy picture of the legal community, most people, at some point in their lives, almost certainly will be presented with various legal problems that will require help.

During the past few years Americans have learned how to take the law into their own hands. Self-help legal books, guides, manuals, and kits are now very popular, especially in family law areas such as wills, divorces, change of name, probate avoidance, adoptions, and many other legal issues. For example, in some states a no-fault divorce can be obtained in some cases merely by filling out a standard form and filing it in court. Some small-claims courts do not permit the parties to use lawyers. You can solve many legal problems without a lawyer if you have adequate information and instructions. In many situations you can avoid legal pitfalls through the effective use of legal guides. Preventive legal care can be as important as preventive medical care. Lawyers, judges, legislative authorities, bar associations, civic organizations, and the general public have recognized, and approved, this trend in our society.

The use of self-help legal guides immediately presents two threshold questions:

- Can you legally represent yourself?
- Should you represent yourself without a lawyer?

Some people erroneously think a lawyer is required for the preparation and execution of a "legal" will; others falsely assume that it is a legal requirement to have a lawyer in court.

You have a legal right to represent yourself. You can be your own lawyer in court and out of court. The critical question is whether you should represent yourself in any particular legal dispute, and, if so, how you can properly prepare to do so. This question might remind you of the proverbial "question in an enigma wrapped up in a puzzle scarred by the twinges of adversity swinging on the rusty hinge of fate."

For those who need legal services but do not hire a lawyer, for whatever reason, it is better to follow the adage of an old football coach, who said, "Do something if you do it wrong — don't just stand there," notwithstanding the apparent efficacy of the old proverb that "one who is his own lawyer has a fool for a client." This age-old dilemma need not result in economic disaster. With the right kind of research and information, and the effective use of legal guides, people can handle most of their legal problems themselves.

In the federal courts, the right of self-representation has been protected by statute since the beginning of our nation.

> In all courts of the United States the parties may plead and conduct their own cases personally or by counsel as, by the rules of such courts, respectively, are permitted to manage and conduct causes therein.[4]

With few exceptions, each of the several states also accords a defendant the right to represent himself in any criminal case. The constitutions of 36 states explicitly confer that right. Moreover, many state courts have expressed the view that the right is also supported by the Constitution of the United States. Indeed, the United States Supreme Court has expressly held that the Sixth Admendment, as made applicable to the states by the Fourteenth Amendment, guarantees to a defendant in a state criminal trial an independent constitutional right of self-representation. The Court also has stated that a defendant may proceed to defend himself without counsel when he voluntarily and intelligently elects to do so. The Court said:

> The Sixth and Fourteenth Amendments of our Constitution guarantee that a person brought to trial in any state or federal court must be afforded the right to the assistance of counsel before he can be validly convicted and punished by imprisonment. This clear constitutional rule has emerged from a series of cases decided here over the last 50 years. The question before us now is whether a defendant in a state criminal trial has a constitutional right to proceed without counsel when he voluntarily and intelligently elects to do so. Stated another way, the question is whether a State may constitutionally hale a person into its criminal courts and there force a lawyer upon him, even when he insists that he wants to conduct his own defense. It is not an easy question, but we have concluded that a State may not constitutionally do so.[5]

---

[4]28 U.S.C. 1654.
[5]Faretta v. California, 422 U.S. 806.

4

The mere fact that you have a legal right to represent yourself in court does not necessarily mean that you should invariably dispense with the services of a lawyer. There are some well-defined cases in which you should have a lawyer's help to get the protection you need, and there are well-defined cases where you might be better off without a lawyer. You be the judge! Indeed, a dissenting judge in the Faretta case observed:

> If there is any truth in the old proverb that 'one who is his own lawyer has a fool for a client,' the court by its opinion today now bestows a constitutional right on one to make a fool of himself.

Another judge said:

> Pro se representation may at times serve the ideal of a fair trial better than representation by an attorney.[6]

In another decision by the U.S. Supreme Court, it was said:

> To deny an accused a choice of procedure in circumstances in which he, though a layman, is as capable as any lawyer of making an intelligent choice, is to impair the worth of great Constitutional safeguards by treating them as empty verbalisms. When the administration of the criminal law . . . is hedged about as it is by the Constitutional safeguards for the protection of an accused, to deny him in the exercise of his free choice that right to dispense with some of these safeguards . . . is to imprison a man in his privilege and call it the Constitution.[7]

Even lawyers have strongly advocated this position. A recent law review article suggests:

> Too often, the bar and the bench have regarded, treated, and disposed of those who proceed without counsel as, at best, outsiders. As a result all parties lose — not only the pro se petitioner, but also those who presume that the pro se petitioner has a worthless claim, or worse, that he himself is

[6]U.S. ex rel Sato v. U.S., 504 F. 2d, 1339.
[7]Adams v. U.S. ex rel McCann, 317 U.S. 260, 279.

somehow worthless because he has no counsel. There are those who recognize that the opportunity to proceed without counsel in our system prevents a strangle-hold on justice by lawyers.[8]

---

[8]"Pro Se Litigation: The Misunderstood Pro Se Litigant. More than a Pawn in the Game," *Brooklyn Law Review* 41:769.

Chapter 2

Avoiding Probate:
The Revocable Living Trust

Probate is the legal process by which property and property rights are transferred from a decedent to others. For many years, the probate system has been dominated and controlled by lawyers and judges. The probate statutes, laws, and procedures have become outdated and out of step with the reality of our modern society. This is one of the primary reasons that motivates people to avoid probate. Many people in this country have become disenchanted with the entire probate process and the mystique that enshrouds it. Americans have been cast into a cloud of darkness as to how to avoid the abuses and scandals of the probate system so frequently reported by the press.

There are several good plans for avoiding probate; however, the plan that is simple, easy, and inexpensive is the revocable living trust. It is so simple and easy to understand and so easy to use that many people who discover it wonder why it is still unknown to so many people.

It is as easy to prepare a revocable living trust as it is a will. This trust involves an agreement by which one party, the *grantor*, transfers property to a trustee to hold for the benefit of another, and is created during the lifetime of the grantor. The grantor retains the right to revoke the trust, change its terms, or regain possession of the trust property. This principle of law is the basis upon which many people avoid all probate processes. Typically, a person can create a revocable living trust in which he is cotrustee with another person—for example, an adult child or partner—to hold and manage the estate. Upon the death of the grantor, there is no probate of the trust property. It is that simple.

The main characteristics of this kind of agreement are that:

- You can cancel it at any time during your life, for any reason, or for no reason
- You retain complete control of your assets
- You can receive all benefits and income
- There are no probate proceedings, no probate delays, no probate expenses, no probate confusion, or intimidation by lawyers
- Your beneficiaries can receive the property immediately
- There is no publicity and no court records or other public proceedings. It is a completely private matter.

You owe it to yourself and your family to explore this plan.

WHAT IS A TRUST?

A *trust* is a legal relationship in which one person transfers property to a second person for the benefit of a third person. The person creating the trust is called the grantor, *trustor*, or *settlor*. The person or entity having legal title to the trust property is the *trustee*, and the person for whose benefit the trust is created is called the *beneficiary*.

The fundamental legal principle you need to understand about a trust is that one person can have two legal entities: as an individual, and as a trustee. For legal, tax, and other purposes, a trustee is a separate person or entity from the person as an individual. Therefore, an individual person can transfer property from his individual name to himself *as Trustee* and hold it for himself or for others. Typically, the Revocable Living Trust Agreement provides that title shall be in the trustee or cotrustees and, upon the death of the grantor, shall go to the designated beneficiary or beneficiaries. When the grantor dies, the property is automatically held by the cotrustee or successor trustee for the beneficiaries without any probate process or court proceedings. This might sound like a bit of legal magic. Indeed, that is exactly what it is: it is an accepted legal fiction to accomplish a noble and worthwhile goal. It avoids probate just as slick as magic.

ELEMENTS OF A TRUST

The four essential elements of a trust are: intention, trust property, trustee, and beneficiary. It is important for you to understand the meaning of these terms in order for you to create your own trust.

Intention. A trust is created only if the grantor properly expresses an intention to create a trust. Generally, a trust can be created by written instrument, by verbal statement, or by conduct. The Statute of Frauds and Statute of Wills require that some transactions be in writing to be enforceable. When the transaction is only oral, the evidence is required to be clear and convincing. No particular form of written words or conduct is necessary. Even though many oral agreements are legal, it is recommended that you always manifest your intentions by a written document, especially in the case of a trust arrangement.

Trust Property. A trust cannot be created unless there is trust property that definitely exists. Any transferable interest, present or future, vested or contingent, legal or equitable, in any object of ownership, tangible or intangible, may be held in trust. This definition would include virtually any kind of property you own.

Trustee. A trust by its very nature requires that there be a trustee to administer it. If, however, you place property in a trust without naming a trustee, or the trustee dies, a court would appoint a trustee to administer the trust. You should be specific in naming a trustee and successor trustees to avoid the unnecessary costs of a court appointment.

As a general rule, any natural person, including the grantor, can hold property in trust in the same way that a person can hold property for his own benefit. Moreover, other entities may act as trustees, such as a bank, a trust company, or a corporation. Where a major objective of a trust is to avoid probate and the excessive fees associated with probate systems, you might wish to avoid naming an attorney, a bank, or a trust company because the fees they charge are an integral part of the probate system.

A property owner may declare himself to be the trustee of property for the benefit of another. In this situation, the property owner is both grantor and trustee. The selection of a trustee other than yourself can be one of the most important aspects of creating a trust. Most people select a close family member, a friend, or a relative. Under the typical Revocable Living Trust Agreement, the only duty of a successor trustee is to convey the trust property to the beneficiaries. If management of a business or other investments are involved, you might wish to consider a person with business experience.

Beneficiary. A private trust, unlike charitable or honorary trusts, requires a beneficiary with the right to enforce it. The beneficiary must either be specifically named or be reasonably ascertained from facts existing at the time the trust is created.

Any person, natural or corporate, who has the capacity to take and hold title to property may be a beneficiary, even though that person might not be capable of administering the property. Indeed, the inability of a beneficiary to manage his own property, as in the case of a minor child, is often a principal reason for creating a trust.

METHODS OF CREATING A TRUST

You can create a trust in several ways:

- By declaring that you hold your property as trustee for yourself and/or others
- By transferring your property to another person as trustee for yourself and/or others
- By transferring, in your will, your property to another person as trustee for others

The third method — by will — is called a *testamentary trust,* and must go through the probate process. You should always use a formal written document when you are creating a trust to avoid any confusion or misunderstanding, and you should not use a testamentary trust if you wish to avoid probate.

The advantages of the revocable living trust include the following:

- Avoiding probate administration fees and expenses
- Avoiding excessive legal fees for probate
- Avoiding unnecessary delays
- Avoiding publicity of probate matters
- Avoiding ancillary administration
- Avoiding statutory restrictions on bequest of property
- Avoiding will contests

- Managing property
- Avoiding interruption of management by incapacity of grantor
- Avoiding the emotional trauma, aggravation, and frustration of a complicated probate process

MARITAL PROPERTY RIGHTS

In most states, the laws give to a surviving spouse certain legal rights that cannot be defeated by will. Some of these state laws, but not all, also give to a surviving spouse certain rights that cannot be defeated by gifts, by a revocable living trust, or by other transfers. These marital property rights are called *community property, dower, courtesy, elective rights, statutory rights,* and various other terms. These rights typically give one-half, one-third, or some other portion of the estate of the decedent to the surviving spouse.

If community property is to be placed in a revocable trust by a married person, the grantor's spouse should join in the execution of the trust agreement. Community property consists of whatever property is gained during the marriage by the toil, talent, or other productive faculty of either spouse. As a general rule, property obtained by one spouse by gift, devise, or descent is not included in community property. You should check the specific laws of your state on this question. The community-property states are Arizona, California, Idaho, Louisiana, New Mexico, Nevada, Texas, and Washington. Marital property rights of spouses vary among other states; therefore, it is suggested that all transfers of property by a married person be signed by the spouse of the grantor. This is not a problem for most married persons because they generally own property in joint names.

The concept behind these laws is that with certain exceptions, property acquired during marriage belongs to both spouses. The marital property rights vary from state to state, and the state laws concerning marital property rights transferred by a Revocable Living Trust Agreement are inconsistent and sometimes difficult to interpret. In general, it is recommended that any married person obtain the consent of the spouse in any trust created during marriage.

The trust doctrine was not fashioned by the courts as an instrument for denying the rights of a spouse. On the contrary, the trust can be used by both married and unmarried persons as an easy, simple, inexpensive way to transfer property from one generation to another without the burdens, delays, expenses, and aggravation of the probate system.

For example, suppose that a married couple provides in a Revocable Living Trust Agreement that all, or a part of, their assets are declared to be held by them, as cotrustees for their benefit during their lifetimes, and upon the death of either spouse to go to the surviving spouse, or in the event of simultaneous deaths to go directly to designated beneficiaries. Immediately upon the death of either spouse, all legal interests in all the property would revert automatically to the surviving spouse, as sole trustee, free and clear from any probate processes or other court delays. The surviving spouse would have the option to place the assets into another revocable living trust with an adult child or other family member as cotrustee and avoid probate again.

Suppose further that an unmarried person provides in a Revocable Living Trust Agreement that all, or a part of, his assets are declared to be held by the grantor and a third party, as cotrustees for the grantor's benefit during his lifetime, and upon the death of the grantor to go to the beneficiaries designated in the agreement. Immediately upon the grantor's death, all legal interests in all the property would revert automatically to the cotrustee, as the sole trustee, to be transferred as directed by the grantor in the agreement. If the beneficiary is an adult, he could be the cotrustee and, upon the grantor's death, he would automatically have title to the property for himself. Easy, simple, legal — all without probate, probate lawyers, judges, and the other trimmings of the probate system.

TRUSTS AND WILLS

The two principal ways you can pass your property to those you want to have it are: by will and by trust. The transfer by will is effective upon the date of death and requires the probate process to make it complete; a transfer by trust avoids the probate proceedings completely. What happens if you do both?

If you leave property to a person in your will and also leave the same property to another person in a revocable living trust, what happens? The trust takes precedence over the will. For example, if you have $100,000 in stocks and first write a valid will leaving the specific stocks to John Doe, and then later execute a revocable living trust transferring the same stocks to Jane Doe, who gets the stocks upon your death? Jane Doe gets the stocks because the trust takes precedence. Suppose further that you first place the stocks in a revocable living trust for John Doe and later execute a valid will leaving the same stocks to Jane Doe. Who gets the stocks upon your death? John Doe gets the stocks. The trust takes precedence over the will whether it was executed before or after the will. Why is this?

The revocable living trust takes precedence over the will in both cases because the title (ownership) of the property was transferred in each transaction when the trust agreement was executed. The title (ownership) to the stocks could not be transferred by will until the death of the owner. Even though you can revoke a trust and you can revoke a will, the trust actually transfers title to the trustee at the time of the execution of the trust. The will does not.

TRANSFERRING TITLE TO PROPERTY

In transferring title to property from a grantor to a trustee, the execution of the trust agreement and listing of the property in Exhibits is legally sufficient for most property. There are, however, various laws and regulations controlling the keeping of records for transfer of some property. You should follow these regulations to ensure that your records are accurate and complete.

Records and Recording Laws. A *public record* is one that is necessary or required by law to be made and kept, or directed by law to serve as memorial and evidence of something written, said, or done. A public record is made by a public officer in pursuance of a duty. Its immediate purpose is to disseminate information to the public or to serve as a memorial of official transactions for public reference.

The system of recording is regulated by statute in each state. The recording requirements might vary from state to state; however, every state has a statutory requirement for the recording of conveyances or transfers of real estate. These records are usually kept at a county seat by a clerk or recorder. The typical statute requires the recording of *all conveyances of real property, deeds, mortgages, deeds of trust, or instruments in the nature of mortgages*, and might include long-term leases, chattel mortgages, mining claims, conveyances on execution, and other matters affecting real property.

The term *conveyance* is defined as some written paper or instrument signed and delivered by one person to another, transferring the title to or creating a lien on property, or giving a right to a debt or duty.

Real Property. If any real property is included in the list of property in Exhibit "A," you should have the trust agreement acknowledged. Also have a separate deed executed transferring the property to the name of the trustee, and have the deed and the trust agreement recorded in the county where the real property is located. You should obtain a real estate deed form in your own state since they vary from state to state. These documents are available at your local real estate offices, law offices, stationery stores, and other convenient places. Since you must record the real property trust, you might want to have separate trusts, one for real property and another for all other property. This method will enable you to record only the real property trust and keep the other matters private in a separate document.

Personal Property. Stocks, bonds, mutual funds, bank accounts, saving and loan accounts, and other similar types of accounts can be included in your trust agreement; however, you need to check with the banks or other financial institutions involved to make appropriate changes in their records and certificates of title, if any.

Automobiles, motorcycles, trailers, and similar kinds of property generally have a certificate of title that is recorded with the appropriate governmental agency. The trustee's name is generally entered on these documents, for example: *John Doe, as Trustee under Revocable Living Trust Agreement dated June 1, 1988.* It is frequently abbreviated as: *John Doe, as Trustee UTD June 1, 1988.*

Some of the financial institutions, especially the banks, might want a copy of the trust agreement in their files. You should check with these institutions and give them directions to make sure your trust agreements will be recognized and that their records are accurate.

In the event you have occasion to transfer additional property to the trust after it has been established or withdraw assets from it, you simply add the new property to Exhibit A and date and sign it, or delete property and date and sign it. Remember, you reserved the right to amend or revoke the trust at any time. If any property is jointly owned, both owners, of course, will need to sign the trust agreement as grantors and also execute any deed or certificate of title.

SELECTION OF TRUSTEES AND SUCCESSOR TRUSTEES

In order to avoid probate, it is generally recommended that the grantor act as trustee or cotrustee. The grantor should consider a cotrustee, especially if an adult beneficiary (for example, spouse or adult child) is a primary or sole beneficiary. A grantor who wants a third-party trustee should consider adult children, other relatives, or business associates. Having a lawyer, trust officer, bank or trust company as trustee defeats one of the major objectives of the trust: avoiding excessive fees and expenses of probate. It is also very important to appoint successor trustees to avoid the expenses, delays, and inconvenience of court appointments.

REVOCATION AND AMENDMENT

The great advantage of the revocable living trust is your ability, at any time, for any reason, or for no reason, to change it or revoke it by the mere stroke of your pen. By using the revocation form, you simply describe the trust agreement you wish to revoke and sign the revocation. If the trust agreement is recorded, you need to record the revocation. Immediately upon your signing the revocation and transmitting it to the trustee, the trust is automatically terminated and revoked as a matter of law. No lawyers, no judges, or lengthy court proceedings are needed. You are in complete control of your property, and it can remain a private matter if you can keep it out of the hands of the probate lawyers.

REVOCABLE LIVING TRUST AGREEMENT FORMS

The essence of avoiding probate via the revocable living trust is simply to transfer title to property to a trustee by a written document. You, the grantor, can maintain complete control, management, and authority over the property. You can revoke at any time if you wish. In other words, the only difference is that you, or another, holds the *legal title* to the property *as Trustee*, and in the event of death the title to the property automatically — as a matter of law — is held as directed in the trust agreement to be used, or transferred, to the beneficiary or beneficiaries you have designated in the agreement. Thus, the *probate* of the assets — transfer through the probate system — is avoided.

The Revocable Living Trust Agreement need not be complicated, complex, or mysterious. Each of the standard provisions of the typical form is discussed and samples given to illustrate how easy it is to prepare a trust.

Introductory Clause. This provision is merely to give the date of the instrument and identify the parties.

> This Revocable Living Trust Agreement is made this _____ day of _____, 19____, between John Doe and Jane Doe, husband and wife, of 123 Main Street, Boulder, Colorado 80301, herein referred to as Grantors, and John Doe and Jane Doe of the City of Boulder, Colorado, herein referred to as cotrustees.

Whereas Clause. This provision states the grantors' intent, which is an essential element of a trust. It identifies the property and states the purpose of the agreement, and the use and disposition of the property.

> Whereas, grantors are now the owners of the property described in Exhibit A attached hereto and made a part hereof, and
>
> Whereas, grantors desire to make provision for the care and management of such property, and the collection of the income therefrom, and the disposition of both such income and such property in the manner herein provided:
>
> Now, therefore, for the reasons set forth above, and in consideration of the mutual convenants set forth herein, grantors and trustees agree as follows:

Transfer of Property. The transfer, or conveyance, of the property is the key to avoiding probate. Because the property is transferred to a trustee, the grantor does not "own" it as a part of his estate to be disposed of in a will.

> Grantors, in consideration of the acceptance by cotrustees of the trust herein created, hereby convey, transfer, assign, and deliver to cotrustees, their successors in trust and assigns, the property described in Exhibit A attached hereto and made a part hereof, by this reference, which property, held by cotrustees hereunder, is herein referred to as Trust

Estate. Grantors, and any other persons, shall have the right at any time to add property acceptable to trustees to this trust and such property, when received and accepted by trustees, shall become a part of the trust estate.

Disposition of Income and Principal. You have a legal right to transfer your property during your lifetime, and after death. You can direct that all such property and all income from that property shall be used by you or anyone else you designate. In the event any beneficiary is a minor, you can direct the trustee to hold the property until the minor reaches majority.

Trustees shall care for and manage the trust estate and collect the income derived therefrom, and, after the payment of all taxes and assessments thereon and all charges incident to the management thereof, dispose of the net income therefrom and corpus thereof, as follows:

During the lifetime of grantors the trustees may pay income of the trust estate and such portions of the principal as the grantors from time to time may direct the grantors, or otherwise as they direct during their lives. After the death of both grantors the successor trustee shall distribute the trust estate to the following beneficiary or beneficiaries who shall survive both grantors:_____ *(Names)*_____

_____.

The share of any beneficiary who shall be under the age of 18 years shall not be paid to such beneficiary but shall instead be held in trust to apply to his/her use all the income thereof, and also such amounts of the principal, even to the extent of all, as the trustees deem necessary or suitable for the support, welfare and education of such beneficiary; and when he/she attains the age of 18 years, to pay him/her the remaining principal, if any. If any beneficiary for whom a share is held in trust should die before having received all the principal thereof, then upon his/her death the remaining principal shall be paid to his/her then living child or children, equally if more than one, and in default thereof, to the then living descendants of the grantors, per stirpes. No interest hereunder shall be transferrable or assignable by any beneficiary, or be subject during his or her life to the claims of his or her creditors. Notwithstanding anything herein to the contrary, the trusts hereunder shall terminate not later than twenty-one (21) years after the death of the last beneficiary named herein.

Revocation and Amendment. You have a legal right to cancel the agreement at any time or change it in any way you desire.

The grantors, or the survivor of them, may, by signed instrument delivered to the trustees, revoke the trusts hereunder, in whole or in part, or amend this Agreement from time to time in any manner.

Successor Trustee. It is important to have a trustee, a co-trustee, or a successor trustee to hold the title after the death of the grantor or grantors. Having a trustee avoids the necessity for a court appointment — a potentially expensive venture into the domain of the probate system.

In the event of the death or incapacity of both cotrustees, we hereby nominate and appoint as successor trustee _____ *(Name)* _____ . In the event the successor trustee does not serve we appoint whomever shall at the time be the first designated beneficiary hereunder. The trustee and their successors shall serve without bond.

Trustees' Acceptance. Since this is an agreement, the other parties, the cotrustees, must agree to the terms of the agreement and sign it.

This trust has been accepted by trustees and will be administered in the State of _____ , and its validity, construction, and all rights hereunder shall be governed by the laws of that state.

Signatures. All grantors and all trustees must sign the agreement. If your state has requirements on recording conveyance documents, review the discussion about *Records and Recording Laws* earlier in this chapter to ensure that the transfer meets all the legal requirements of your state recording laws.

In Witness Whereof, grantors and trustees have executed this Agreement on the date above written.

_____*(Signature)*_____	_____*(Signature)*_____
Grantor	Cotrustee
_____*(Signature)*_____	_____*(Signature)*_____
Grantor	Cotrustee
_____*(Signature)*_____	
Witness (1)	
_____*(Signature)*_____	
Witness (2)	

Sworn to and subscribed before me this _____ day of _____, 19____.

_____*(Signature)*_____
Notary Public

Exhibit A Schedule of Property. Exhibit A is the place for listing and specifically identifying the property that is the subject of the trust. Make sure you use the legal description of real estate to avoid any doubts about the transfer of title on the record.

There are other provisions you can use in the agreements, depending upon the facts and circumstances of your particular situation, but these are the essential parts for avoiding probate. If you have any difficulty in completing the Trust Agreement and the other documents, you might wish to obtain assistance from a real estate broker or an attorney.

Chapter 3

Other Methods and Techniques for Avoiding Probate

The revocable living trust is the "classic" method for avoiding probate; however, there are a number of other methods and techniques you can use in your estate planning to avoid the pain and anguish of the probate system. These methods are easy to use, and you do not need a lawyer. These plans sometimes have been referred to as *substitute wills*, in the sense that an owner of property is able to transfer property to others without having it go through the probate system. The term *substitute will* is not literally correct, however, because probate is avoided only with respect to the specific property that is included in a probate avoidance plan; all other assets owned by a decedent would be subject to probate. Most people need a will in addition to probate avoidance plans because they do not generally wish to have all their property in a trust or other probate avoidance program. This is not to suggest that these people cannot avoid probate with respect to "everything" they own, but there are some general guidelines to be followed in determining who should avoid probate and for what property.

Who should avoid probate with respect to what property depends upon the particular facts and circumstances of each case. In general, it is recommended that persons who are settled in their estate, family, and financial affairs should implement probate avoidance plans. Settled in *affairs* is an expression that refers generally to people in any of the following categories:

- They own capital assets that can easily be held in trust or other probate avoidance plans
- Their children are no longer minors
- They have reached middle age
- They have substantial assets
- They simply want to save 10 to 20 percent or more of an estate for their family, rather than permitting it to be churned through the probate processes.

Probate avoidance is accomplished by placing title to property in such a way that upon the death of the owner, it legally passes to another who holds it outside the jurisdiction of the probate courts. In addition to the revocable living trust, this can be accomplished by:

- Joint Ownership, with right of survivorship
- Gifts
- Life Insurance (payable to beneficiaries other than the insured or the insured's estate)
- The Irrevocable Living Trust

JOINT OWNERSHIP

The joint ownership of property with right of survivorship is one of the easiest ways to avoid probate. The jointly owned property automatically becomes that of the survivor or survivors as a matter of law, and no probate is needed. The joint ownership method can be effective with real estate as well as other property, such as bank accounts, mutual funds, stocks, bonds, automobiles, and antiques. It is important for you to comply with any title certificate or recording requirements of your state. For example, registering automobile certificates or recording real estate conveyances must comply with local recording laws.

Although every state authorizes some form of joint ownership with right of survivorship, the terminology might differ from state to state. As a result, in order to convey real property titles, you will want to use printed real estate forms designed for your particular state.

In most states, this method of title ownership is called Joint Tenancy, with right of survivorship. A few states call it an *Estate by the Entirety* when used as between husband and wife. Eight states have community property laws, and property held by husband and wife in those states is governed by the community-property principles.

Joint Tenancy, with Right of Survivorship (JTWROS). An estate in joint tenancy is one held by two or more persons jointly, with equal rights to share in its enjoyment during their lives. It has as its distinguishing feature the right of survivorship, or *jus accrescendi*, by virtue of which the entire estate, upon the death of a joint tenant, goes to the survivor or, in the case of more than two joint tenants, to the survivors, and so on to the last survivor, free and exempt of all charges made by the deceased.

One of the great advantages of the doctrine of survivorship is that a joint tenant cannot devise (leave by a will) interests in the land, because of three provisions: the device does not take effect until after the death of the decedent; the claim of the surviving tenant arises in the same instant as that of the devisee; and the interests of a joint tenant have priority by law over those of a devisee. It is equally clear that the interests of the deceased joint tenant cannot descend to his heirs or pass to his representatives under the laws regulating intestate succession. A surviving joint tenant holds his right under the conveyance or instrument by which the tenancy was created, and not under laws regulating intestate succession. Furthermore, the creditors of a deceased joint tenant do not have any recourse against the surviving joint tenant who acquires the property under the conveyance.

At common law and also under the law as it generally prevails at present, the creation and the continued existence of a joint tenancy depend upon the coexistence of four requisites:

- The tenants must have one and the same interests
- The interests must accrue by one and the same conveyance
- They must commence at one and the same time
- The property must be held by one and the same undivided possession.

In other words, there must be the following four entities: unity of interest, unity of title, unity of time, and unity of possession. If any one of these elements is lacking, the estate will not be in joint tenancy.

In most states, these principles have been codified and are

regulated by statute. If you have any doubts, you should check the specific statutes of your own state. All natural persons can be involved in such an estate, and in most states other entities can be joint tenants.

Although most people think of joint tenancy as confined to interests in real property, a joint tenancy of such character can exist in any kind of property. Joint ownership of bank accounts, savings accounts, brokerage accounts, and other such titles are regulated by statutes in most states, and you can easily find out about these laws from your financial institutions. It is recommended that you discuss the subject with a financial officer in the institutions where you do business to make certain that they understand, and comply with, your desires and instructions. Do not depend upon a bank, insurance company, or other financial institution to arbitrarily do your estate planning by blindly following some interoffice memo or procedure manual. You should direct them to record your account exactly as you want it.

Tenancy in Common. You should not confuse a joint tenancy with right of survivorship with a tenancy in common. They are, legally, very different. *Tenancy in Common* is a tenancy whereby two or more persons are entitled to land in such manner that they have an undivided possession, but several freeholds or interests. In a tenancy in common, which is not limited to husband and wife, there is no right of survivorship. Each owns undivided interests in the property. Either coowner may dispose of his undivided interest in the property during his life, or by will. When one coowner dies, his interest (an undivided interest) does not go to the surviving coowner, but to the decedent's heirs or according to will. Therefore, this kind of ownership does not avoid probate.

Tenancy by the Entirety. A tenancy by the entirety, or estate by the entirety, exists (in some states) only where the coowners are husband and wife. When either spouse dies, the survivor becomes the sole owner by right of survivorship. The right of survivorship cannot be destroyed during the lives of the coowners except with the consent of both. In some states, this form of ownership exists only with respect to real property; in a few states it might exist in the case of personal property. For historical reasons, the term *estate by the entirety* is used in some states, but the legal effect is the same as the joint tenancy, with right of survivorship.

COMMUNITY PROPERTY

Community property, applicable in eight states, is property owned in common by husband and wife, each having an undivided one-half interest by reason of their marital status. The eight states with community property laws are Arizona, California, Idaho, Louisiana, Nevada, New Mexico, Texas, and Washington. The other states are governed by common law principles. *Community property* is the property that remains after family living expenses and all other community debts have been paid. It is said to be a fundamental postulate of the community-property system that whatever is gained during coverture, by the toil, talent, or other productive faculty of either spouse, is community property. Community property, under the statutes, usually includes all property acquired by either spouse during a marriage, other than by gift, devise, or descent.

GIFTS

Property that you give away is no longer a part of your estate for probate purposes; therefore you avoid probate with respect to that property. Gift taxes could be assessed; however, there is an unlimited exemption for spouses, and a $10,000 exclusion annually per donee. Gifts can be used as an estate planning tool for avoiding probate, and with proper planning no gift or estate taxes will be assessed.

LIFE INSURANCE

Generally, life insurance is payable directly to the designated beneficiaries and is not a part of an estate for probate purposes. Moreover, you can avoid estate taxes on insurance if you and your estate do not retain any ownership or interest in the insurance contract. Typically, you can have your spouse or other family member own life insurance policies on your life, and it does not become a part of your estate for probate purposes or for tax purposes.

IRREVOCABLE LIVING TRUST

An irrevocable living trust, as its name indicates, is one that cannot be revoked or changed. It is final. There are some tax advantages in using an irrevocable trust, and it also has most of the advantages of a revocable trust. This trust can be used for gifts, typically to minors. The assets in an irrevocable trust will avoid the probate system, avoid estate taxes in some circumstances, and avoid income taxes to the grantor. Also, the trustee can manage the property for the beneficiaries, if needed.

Chapter 4

How To Handle Probate

Our probate laws were originally formulated in England at a time when there was very little mobility for most people and estates were largely composed of land or property affixed to land. The development of our probate laws in early America also evolved at a time when there was relatively little mobility in our society. In modern times, however, with a highly mobile society in which families typically live in many different states, own property of all kinds in many different states, and are constantly traveling, the probate laws have become so out of touch with contemporary reality that they represent little more than an obstacle that must be overcome before an estate can be settled.

Unfortunately, it is almost always modest estates or inheritances that get caught up in the majestic spider web of the probate processes. These modest estates are usually even smaller or nonexistent by the time they escape from the jaws of the probate trap with its extravagant fees, unending delays, and probate costs.

When a person dies, he is no longer able to exercise dominion or control over the property he owned or controlled. Through proper estate planning prior to death, a person may direct, and articulate with particularity, what shall and shall not be done with his estate.

If a person wants to dispose of his property by will, as permitted under the law, the property must pass according to the terms of a valid will. If, on the other hand, a person leaves no will, the statutes of each state, through the laws of descent and distribution, provide for the transfer of the property to the persons designated in the statutes.

In either event — by will or by statutory law — the passing of the property is accomplished by a court drama called probate proceedings, or the probate process. Probate can be avoided through good estate planning.

DO YOU NEED A LAWYER?

One of the false notions that has developed in this country is that, when a person dies, the family and heirs must automatically hire a lawyer to handle the probate.

If you or some member of your family should become a prospective executor or administrator, and most of us are, you should calmly and dispassionately learn all about the probate system in your state. Talk to the clerk or other personnel at the local probate court. Get a copy of the local probate rules and statutes. Review the probate steps listed later in this chapter, after which you will probably know whether you need a lawyer. If, after completing these procedures, you have serious doubts, you should talk with your lawyer.

The most important advice I can give you at this point is: do not assume all lawyers can do a good job in probate matters. Investigate the local lawyers to find one who is honest and competent. After you hire a lawyer, it is to your advantage to learn as much as possible about the proceedings so that you can assist your lawyer in saving time, fees, and additional costs.

We are quick to criticize lawyers; however, a great part of the excessive fees, delays, and confusion is caused by the clients themselves. As an employer of the lawyer, you can control the entire probate process if you understand it. If you do not know what is going on, you not only contribute to wasted time, inefficiency, and excessive costs, but you might cause dissension and hostility between you and your lawyer. If the lawyer must spend a lot of time explaining many of the probate procedures to you, the estate will lose money, and if the lawyer must do your job, it will result in additional expenses.

You can handle many of the probate steps yourself, with or without a lawyer. The more items you complete, the lower the legal fees. At $75.00 to $200.00 or more per hour, this can result in considerable savings for you. Moreover, many of the probate steps should be done by executors, not lawyers. Perhaps the most satisfying thing about learning all about the probate process is that you will not be intimidated by an overbearing lawyer.

Although the question as to whether you need a lawyer in any particular case is largely a fact question depending on what is involved, there are some serious issues involved in the area of unauthorized practice of law. As discussed in Chapter 1, every individual in America has a legal right to represent himself in court.

Some state constitutions are to the same effect. However, you might not, as an executor or administrator, have a right to represent the estate in probate court. In other words, you cannot practice law without a license, yet you may handle many of the routine matters that do not constitute the practice of law, but that many estates pay lawyers to do.

The general rule is stated as follows:

> Whether an executor or administrator is required to be represented by an attorney in probate court may, in some degree, depend upon the complexity of the legal questions presented in the particular situation. In some instances a lay fiduciary may be considered as attempting to practice law when he deals with legal estate problems in a resprestative capacity, by appearing in probate court on behalf of the estate. In the few cases which have been found on the subject, it has generally been recognized that where the duties of an administrator or executor take on the appearance of the practice of law, as may well be the case in a representative appearance in probate court, representation by counsel is required. However, at least one case has allowed a corporate fiduciary to be represented by law employees in probate court, insofar as the handling of matters of an "administrative" nature is concerned. Another exception to the general requirement of representation by counsel may arise in a situation in which the personal rights of the executor or administrator are concerned.[1]

---

[1]"Necessity that Executor or Administrator Be Represented By Counsel in Presenting Matters in Probate," *American Law Reports*, 19, 3rd Ed.:1104.

HOW DO YOU SELECT A LAWYER?

Although a vast majority of lawyers are honest and competent, only a small percentage are experts in probate matters. Honesty and competency in a lawyer might not be sufficient qualifications for your case. If a case involves anything more than routine matters, which you can probably do yourself, you should retain a lawyer who has experience in probate matters. Once you determine that you may need to retain a lawyer, you should recognize that one of your important legal duties to the estate is to choose a good lawyer, not just any lawyer. The work, time, investigation, and research you put into the selection of a good lawyer can result in great benefits to the estate in the long run.

One of your best sources of information is the probate judge and the probate staff. Many authors suggest you ask your friends, neighbors, and associates about lawyers, but they generally will not know any more than you do. Moreover, you should base your selection more on facts than on hearsay or the opinions of friends.

After you make a list of the experienced probate lawyers in town, you can check the probate files to see just how prior proceedings were handled by the lawyers you are considering. This is also an excellent opportunity to get a feel for what a probate file looks like. Do not be timid about asking a lawyer about his experience, expertise, and qualifications. Your careful questioning of the lawyer about his qualifications will indicate to him that you are an informed client who wants action, competency, and efficiency, and that you will not tolerate delays, incompetence, or exorbitant fees. Finally, after you find the right lawyer, make sure that you have a complete understanding about fees, and put your agreement in writing.

Since you will know many of the steps involved in probate proceedings, you can tell the lawyer in advance that you can do some of the work yourself, thereby saving the lawyer's time and cutting down on fees. In discussing fee arrangements, many lawyers will casually say, "Oh, well, don't worry about it; we'll just charge the statutory fee." Don't do it! Do not routinely agree to any statutory fee or any other so-called standard fee schedule. These so-called statutory fees are not mandatory in most instances (except that most judges automatically award them as a minimum), and if the estate is fairly large, the fee schedule indicated in most state statutes is likely to be excessive. Also reject any suggestion that "We'll just let the judge decide the fees."

Make certain that you fully understand the fee agreement, that it is in writing, and that you have a copy of it. Do not let the lawyer get out of control. If any dispute should develop about the fees, you can always present the question to the judge. Moreover, if you have to hire a second lawyer to fight the first lawyer about fees, you are on a sinking ship.

One final tip: In many cases, probate is unnecessary, especially if the decedent does a little estate planning. In addition, your state might have an informal procedure in which you may not need a lawyer.

WHAT ARE THE DUTIES OF AN EXECUTOR?

One of the most elusive things about the probate process that most people who have an interest in the probate of an estate (surviving spouses, executors, heirs, devisees, etc.) do not realize is that most of the work involved is not legal work and does not require a lawyer. If you follow the checklist in this chapter, you will save a great deal of time, money, and frustration simply by knowing what is to be done, who should do it, and how you can keep control over the activities of your lawyer.

Everything you do will save on legal fees, and knowing what should and should not be done by lawyers also will result in great savings for the estate. Your understanding of the procedures will enable you to avoid a lot of the unnecessary work that most probate lawyers routinely do to increase their fees.

It is recommended that you review these step-by-step procedures (not all are involved in all estates) and do your own research. You then will be able to do your job efficiently, effectively, and competently, and require the same from your lawyer.

Before Probate Proceedings

The following work should be done by an executor or administrator, not a lawyer.

1. Notice of Decease. Give notice to all banks, savings and loan associations, credit unions, brokerage accounts, financial institutions, and other businesses where the decedent has accounts or business relationships. Obtain passbooks, certificates, factual data, and all other information about the accounts. It also might be appropriate, depending on the family situation, to give notices to friends and business associates. Later, if probate proceedings are instituted, the statutes of your state may require a formal notice to be published.

2. Insurance. Check insurance coverage on all of the decedent's estate, including property, casualty, and life insurance. It will be necessary to determine all coverage for the purposes of protecting assets, changing insurance coverage as appropriate, and assisting in making claims on life coverage.

It might be appropriate in some situations to change the name of the insured from the decedent's name to the name of the estate. In other situations, where title to property passes on to the beneficiaries, it might be appropriate to wait and transfer the insurance coverage along with title to the property.

Although life insurance is generally payable directly to the beneficiaries, it might be appropriate for an executor to assist the beneficiaries in the settlement of insurance claims. If life insurance proceeds are a part of the estate for tax purposes, it might be necessary for an executor to make proper tax returns.

3. Mail. Notify the post office and arrange for receipt of the decedent's mail. It is also generally appropriate when you notify friends and business associates to request that mail be addressed directly to you instead of to the decedent.

4. Copy of Will. Make additional copies of the decedent's will, if any, for beneficiaries, taxing authorities, and others who might need it. You will be surprised to learn how many people have some interest or claim in estates and want a copy of the will. You also will be surprised at the number of people who show a great surprise at being left out of a will. Of course, copies of the will are obtainable from the probate court, but it is much easier and less expensive to have extra copies available.

5. Copies of Death Certificate. Make several copies of the death certificate, since it will be needed in many of the transactions connected with the collection of the property, and the management and distribution of the estate. Extra copies will be needed for social security, insurance claims, bank transactions, and many other items.

6. Family Conference. Schedule a family conference at which all interested parties can be advised of the facts available and exchange information and ideas about the handling of the estate. This could be one of the most important things you will do in the administration of an estate. The more you know about what needs to be done and who should do it, the more you will gain the confidence of the beneficiaries, family members, and others who are interested in the estate. Again, it is important that you learn about the probate process before you are thrust into the role of executor or administrator without any idea of what you will be required to do.

A number of subjects should be discussed at these meetings. Discretion is required as to how many meetings to hold, who attends, what is discussed, and what is done. If you handle these meetings in an efficient manner by being prepared with a checklist of things to be done and suggestions as to who should do what, you not only will gain the confidence of all those involved, but you can save a lot of potential conflicts and friction among family members.

You should determine in advance of this meeting what topics should be avoided, what can be accomplished, and how it can be accomplished. One of the most critical items to take care of is the immediate needs of the surviving spouse and close family members.

7. Burial Arrangements. Social Security or veterans benefits are sometimes involved in making burial arrangements. Rarely will an executor be appointed by the court before the funeral; therefore, it is generally some member of the family who will assist in making burial arrangements — sometimes under great stress and intimidation. Proper estate planning by the decedent can greatly facilitate what otherwise might be a very complex and expensive ordeal.

8. Consider Employment of Attorney. The family conference is a good time to discuss if you need to employ an attorney, and if so, who. If the decedent has a regular attorney who assisted in the estate planning, the choice might be easy. In a vast majority of the cases, however, the decedent not only does not have an attorney, he most likely did not have any significant estate plans or other activities designed to make the administration of the estate easier.

You might need to delay a decision as to whether or not a lawyer is needed until you learn more about the estate. There have been many situations where a surviving family retained an attorney to probate an estate only to learn later that no probate was needed. This is not only expensive and awkward; it can be embarrassing for the attorney and for those who retain him. If there are any assets, however, most lawyers will go to work whether they are needed or not.

9. Safe Deposit Boxes. List the contents of any safe deposit boxes in the decedent's name. Most state laws provide that certain persons must be present at opening, including tax authorities, and that an inventory must be made of all the contents of safe deposit boxes. After the box is opened, its contents are listed, and you have proper approval, you can take possession of all valuables and make sure that they are properly protected and distributed.

10. Preliminary Estimate of Estate Property. Make a preliminary estimate of the decedent's estate to determine what form the probate and administration of the estate should take. This is the point at which it might first become evident that the estate is small enough to come within the no-probate provisions of the statutes. You should research these provisions as soon as you get a copy of your state statute.

11. Collection and Protection of Property.

a. Search the household, make an inventory of all personal property, and arrange for storage and protection of personal property. Discretion is required where there is a surviving spouse who is living in the home. In fact, you might have very little to do with personal tangible property in this situation. Do not interfere where you are not required by law to do so. Moreover, most decedents and their survivors do not want unnecessary "poking around" by lawyers or executors where it is not necessary.

Real estate protection and management is of particular importance where the decedent owned apartments, business buildings, or other real estate that needs day-to-day management. A going business usually requires immediate attention, unless there is a surviving partner or manager.

b. The title to automobiles in the decedent's name can be especially troublesome. For example, family members usually will want to drive an automobile, but the estate might be liable for any accident in which the automobile is involved. You should make sure all cars have proper insurance coverage, and either sell the cars for cash or transfer the title to beneficiaries as soon as possible.

c. The decedent's checkbooks and bank records might be the greatest source of information about the financial transactions in which he was involved. Moreover, they will be essential for later use in preparing tax returns.

d. All cash owned by the decedent (and not jointly owned by a surviving spouse) should be accounted for, used for estate obligations, put to work, or distributed to the persons who are entitled to receive it.

e. Lease houses, apartments, offices, business buildings, equipment, or other property. If the living facilities of a decedent become vacant, it is essential to avoid losses and damages through failure to properly protect and manage the property. Where business property is not being managed by a surviving spouse or partner, it is important to take quick action in disposing of the property or obtaining competent management. Make sure that there is adequate insurance coverage on all property.

f. Transfer title, if appropriate, to personal property. If the estate is uncomplicated and the probate is not delayed, you probably will wish to transfer title to most personal property directly to the beneficiaries (for example, automobiles, stocks, mutual funds). If, however, you anticipate delays, complex or extended litigation, tax claims, or other conflicts that will require a long probate process, you might wish to transfer title to income-producing property to the estate. This is a matter of discretion and will depend on the facts in each case. In all events, you should be alert to the problems involved and be prepared to solve them without unnecessary confusion or delay.

g. Collect rents, interest, dividends, royalties, debts, etc. Until you can complete the administration of an estate, it will be your duty to take care of all financial transactions involving the assets of the estate. You might be required to institute legal action to collect some of the debts owed to the decedent or to the estate.

h. Assemble data on all property owned by the decedent that will not be a part of the probate estate. Jointly owned property, trust property, life insurance proceeds, and other assets might be a part of the taxable estate for tax purposes only, and pass directly to others without any probate proceedings. Where tax problems occur, it will be part of your duty to prepare tax returns that reveal all the facts, including the value and aggregate amounts.

i. Appoint appraisers. It might be necessary to have appraisers appointed in the sale or disposition of some of the assets. Do not assume that all appraisers are competent — or honest. You should carefully review the qualifications of any appraiser appointed and be sure you have a fee arrangement in writing.

12. Utilities, Charge Accounts, Credit Cards, etc. A large number of business activities of a decedent, including credit cards, should be closed down as soon as possible. You might want to transfer some accounts into the name of the estate; for example, utilities, telephone, and other services that are needed by you, the family, or business. Otherwise, it is appropriate to close out the accounts of a decedent or have them transferred to the surviving spouse or other family members.

13. Employer Benefits, Salary, Bonuses, Pension and Profit Sharing Plans, etc. Many of the decedent's personal matters might be handled by the surviving spouse or other family members; however, it is usually appropriate and proper for an executor to assist in most of these matters.

14. Open Estate Bank Accounts. If the probate is complicated or, for other reasons, might last a long time, you probably will need a bank account in the name of the estate so you can carry on the financial transactions necessary to bring the estate to a close. Generally, these transactions will not occur until after probate proceedings are filed and you are officially appointed as executor.

15. Personal Records and Tax Returns. You should assemble all personal records and tax returns of the decedent in order to familiarize yourself with all the financial transactions involved. These records will be essential for obtaining the background information and facts you will need to handle the estate properly and to prepare tax returns.

16. Social Security, Civil Service, Veterans, and Other Benefits. These are also items that might be more of a personal problem for the surviving members of the family. They are, however, frequently handled by an executor, or most frequently by an attorney, who charges high fees for nonlegal work that any layman could do.

17. Family Allowance and Assistance. Each state statute has a provision for family allowances pending probate of an estate. You can get preliminary information on these items at the first family conference.

18. Going Business. Obtain all information about any partnership agreements, buy-sell agreements, or other business arrangements of the decedent.

Check any litigation, claims, or other controversies relating to the decedent's property or property interests. In the case of a going business, quick action is needed to manage the business yourself or to obtain competent management personnel.

19. Current Bills and Obligations. Early in the probate process, you should formulate some estimates as to whether the estate is solvent or potentially insolvent. If you are sure the estate is solvent, you might wish to pay current bills and obligations to avoid interest and penalties. If, however, questions remain as to the estate's solvency, you should be cautious about making any payments on estate obligations. In most situations, it might be appropriate to require a claimant to file a claim in the probate proceedings; however, telephone bills, utility bills, and the like might need to be paid to avoid termination of services.

Probate Proceedings Step by Step

1. Employment of Attorney. After you hold a family conference and complete the preliminary estimate of the assets of the estate, you will be in a position to know whether or not an attorney should be employed to assist in the probate court. If no probate is necessary, you generally can forget about retaining a lawyer. Furthermore, in situations where most of the property was jointly owned and there are no tax problems or litigation, a lawyer is not needed. If most of the property passes outside probate and there are no estate tax problems, there is no need for a lawyer. You will be surprised to learn how much you can do yourself — and how much you can save in legal fees — if you review the statutes and court rules with the idea of doing the things you are permitted to do as executor or administrator.

2. Determine If Probate Is Not Necessary. Your preliminary estimate of assets and your first review of your state statute will enable you to determine if probate is unnecessary, usually without the need for a lawyer's advice. In a vast majority of cases, a lawyer is not needed. Moreover, unless some conflict or controversy arises, there is virtually nothing for a lawyer to do in a small estate (other than performing the executor's work at a high cost to the estate).

36

3. Preliminary Information.

a. Determine the domicile of the decedent for probate purposes.

b. Determine the place of administration and possibility of ancillary probate in other states. Avoid probate in other states, if possible.

c. Determine what kind of probate is appropriate — formal, informal, etc. Keep this question in mind when you first review your state statutes.

4. Initial Proceedings in Court.

a. Offer the will for probate or apply for administration — formal or informal.

b. Obtain Letters Testamentary or Letters of Administration. Get extra copies of these documents for banks, claims, and other transactions.

c. Arrange for bonds, if required.

d. Publish any notice required by statutes or rules.

e. Publish notice to creditors.

5. Arrange for Ancillary Administration, if Required.

6. Prepare and File Inventory.

7. Tax Aspects of Estate Administration. Although you might need an accountant to assist in the preparation of tax returns, you should become familiar with all the necessary forms and the instructions for completing them. These can be obtained from IRS offices. It is recommended that you get a copy of *IRS Publication 559, Federal Tax Guide for Survivors, Executors and Administrators*, and other information on tax requirements for an estate.

Some of the usual requirements that you need to know include the following:

a. Apply for tax identification number

b. File Income Tax Return, Form 1040 for decedent

c. File Form 712, Life Insurance Statement

d. File Fiduciary Income Tax Return, Form 1041

e. File Estate Tax Return

f. File U.S. Quarterly Gift Tax Return

8. Claims Against the Estate. Legitimate claims should be paid as soon as reasonably possible to avoid interest and penalties, provided the estate is solvent and has funds available. You should investigate all estate claims to make sure that they are valid. In the event litigation develops, your lawyer can handle it

for you, but you can assist by having available all facts, evidence, and witnesses.

9. Distribution of the Estate.

a. Pay all taxes due.

b. Pay all costs, expenses, fees, and other administration costs of probate.

c. Satisfy all claims against the estate.

d. Pay family allowances.

e. Satisfy specific bequests.

f. Satisfy general bequests.

g. Distribute residuary to beneficiaries.

10. Accounting. Records must be kept of all transactions so you can account to beneficiaries, tax authorities, and the court, and have a final accounting of all assets.

11. Order of Discharge. After completion of all acts necessary to conclude the probate proceedings, file you application for an order of discharge. This marks an end to the probate proceedings.

Chapter 5

How To Write Your Own Will

A vast majority of the people in this country do not have a valid will. Many are reluctant to discuss wills because they seem to equate a will with death, tragedy, and trauma. Few women have a valid will, and most married women do not know anything about the wills and estate planning, if any, of their husbands. This reluctance to talk about wills or engage in proper estate planning and will writing can result in tragedy for many people who are well qualified to prepare a proper, adequate, and valid will. It is extremely important for every adult to be able to analyze his own personal assets and family situation, to be able to review his own estate planning, and to be able to prepare and execute a valid will without being intimidated by lawyers, many of whom are more interested in telling you about their ideas than in listening to yours.

Psychologically and emotionally we all tend to feel that talking about wills, taxes, and death is unpleasant, sad, and distressing. If your loved ones are to be protected, however, it is vital that you learn all about wills. You should know what might happen if you do not have a will. You should be aware of the liabilities of having a badly planned estate or a badly drafted will, and you should know how to minimize taxes and how to prepare a valid will.

You probably do realize the importance of having a will, and if you already have one, you probably know the importance of reviewing it periodically to accommodate any changes in your estate, changes in your family relationships, or tax savings to which you and your family are entitled under the law.

This chapter will enable you to learn how simple and easy it is for you to write your own will without needing to incur excessive and unnecessary legal fees. I became very distressed during the many years of my law practice at seeing so many probate proceedings that were "rip-offs" by probate lawyers. Some of the worst tragedies resulted from poorly planned estates or failure to properly prepare wills. The knowledge and information in this chapter will help you in many ways, in addition to writing your own will.

With or without a will, the probate process can be tragic for most participants if you do not have a competent probate lawyer. A valid will, however, can avoid a lot of trouble, wasted time, expenses, frustration, and intimidation from the legal community.

Even if you choose to have your lawyer assist you in preparing your will, you should learn all about wills, estate planning, and probate laws because you should not be intimidated by lawyers, and you should not have to pay exorbitant fees for something you can do yourself. You will be pleasantly surprised to learn how easy it is to write your own will. Although most people think a will is mysterious, complicated, and filled with serious legal problems, it is really a very simple task.

WHAT IS A WILL?

A *will* is an instrument executed by a competent person in the manner prescribed by statutes, whereby he makes a disposition of his property to take effect on and after his death. To be a will, a document must be testamentary in character and must be executed in accordance with the requirements of the applicable state statute. An instrument is *testamentary* in character if, from the language used, it is apparent that the writer intended to make a disposition of his property, or some part of it, to be effective at death. In the absence of testamentary intent (*animus testandi*), there is no will. It is, of course, essential that a testator know and understand the contents of his will. A disposition of property is not a requirement of a will, even though it is generally the main reason most people write a will. A person might make a will for the sole purpose of nominating an executor, or appointing a guardian.

A will must be *ambulatory*, that is, subject to change, and revocable during the maker's lifetime. The Latin phrase, *ambulatoria voluntas*, a changeable will, denotes the power that a testator possesses of altering his will during his lifetime. The term *testament*, in early common law days, referred only to a disposition of personal property, and the term *will* referred only to a disposition of real property; but in modern usage, the term *will* includes every kind of testamentary act taking effect from the mind of the testator and manifested by an instrument in writing executed and attested in conformity to the statutes. Any writing, however informal it is, that is made with the intent to dispose of property at the death of the writer, if executed in accordance with the statutory requirements, might be a good testamentary disposition. A letter, post card, memo, informal notes on envelopes, and other informal writings might constitute a will if they have the essential elements of a will. Also, as we shall see later, it is not essential in all states to have a will witnessed if certain other requirements are met.

A *nuncupative will* is one that is not in writing, and exists only when the testator, without any writing, declares his will orally before witnesses. A *holographic will*, discussed later, is one that is entirely written and signed (and in some states, dated) by the testator in his own handwriting. Holographic wills are valid in 23 states.

A *codicil* is some addition to, qualification of, or change of a will. *Bequest* means a gift of real property by will. A devisor devises real property, and a devisee is one who takes property by a devise.

An *acknowledgment* is a formal declaration before an authorized official, by a person who executed an instrument, that it is his free act and deed. An *executor* (man) or *executrix* (woman) is the personal representative of a decedent leaving a will. A *guardian* is a person lawfully vested with the power, and charged with the duty, of taking care of a person and managing the property rights of another person, who for some peculiarity of status or defect of age, understanding, or self-control is considered incapable of administering his own affairs. *Intestate* is the status of one who dies without a will. A *testator* (man) or *testatrix* (woman) is one who dies leaving a will. The words *execution, subscribe*, and *subscription* simply mean the signing of an instrument, usually at the end of it. In some states, it is an absolute statutory requirement that a will be signed at the end.

Attestation consists of witnessing the execution of the will by the testator in order to see and take notes mentally that those things are done which the statute requires for the execution of a will, and that the signature of the testator exists as a fact. The primary purpose of requiring a will to be attested is to render available proof that there has been a compliance with the statutory requisites of the execution of a will, and that the instrument offered for probate is the exact paper the alleged testator signed, and not a surreptitious will, fraudulently substituted.

Publication of a will consists in the communication by the testator to the attesting witnesses at the time they attest the instrument of his intention that it shall take effect as his will.

WHAT IS A SIMPLE WILL?

As a general rule, a one- or two-page will is entirely adequate for most people, married or unmarried. The term *simple will* is broadly and generally used in legal circles to describe a will for any person who does not have significant estate tax problems or legal entanglements requiring special provisions. Under the new tax code, estate taxes generally do not become a problem until the estate exceeds $600,000. Lawyers are sometimes reluctant to refer to a client's will as simple because they do not want the client to think his estate is small, and might not want the client to get the impression that the client's will is easy to prepare. For our purposes, we will use the term *basic will* to describe the great majority of wills for estates having no significant estate tax problems and no unusual legal entanglements. This covers the vast majority. Essentially, in the absence of major tax or legal problems, the purpose of a will is rather basic: simply to appoint an executor and make a disposition of property.

The basic will avoids the inconvenience and uncertainty of intestacy. It also allows you to appoint an executor to handle the administration of the estate, rather than having a probate judge appoint one. Moreover, you can minimize the expenses of administration by waiving bonds in appropriate circumstances. Additional savings result from your appointment of an executor or guardian because if you fail to do so, there probably will be legal fees incurred in the proceedings to have the probate court make appointments. It also will cause some delays in most cases. Most married persons, with or without children, generally wish to have the entire estate go to the surviving spouse. This may not happen if you do not have a will. The basic will also makes provision for appointment of a guardian for minor children in the event of simultaneous deaths or where a spouse is predeceased, and a provision for a trust for minors. Thus, the basic will is all that is needed by most people.

In the event your estate exceeds $600,00 or is involved in legal entanglements, you should consult with your lawyer. Of course, married persons have no estate taxes on amounts left to surviving spouses.

HOLOGRAPHIC WILLS

Some state statutes permit a person to write a valid holographic will in his own handwriting with no witnesses needed; some states do not. Some of the statutes require that the will be written, dated, and signed entirely in the testator's own handwriting. Other statutes, based on the Uniform Probate Code, require only that the signature and the material provisions of the will be in the testator's handwriting. By requiring only the material provisions to be in the testator's handwriting, such holographic wills might be valid even though immaterial parts, such as the date or introductory wording, are printed or stamped. Under these statutes, a valid holographic will might even be executed on some printed will forms if the printed portion could be eliminated and the handwritten portion could evidence the testator's will. For some persons unable to obtain legal assistance, the holographic will might be adequate.

The holographic will as a distinct type originated in French law. Express provision for it was made in the Code of Napoleon, which provided:

A holographic testament shall not be valid, unless it be written entirely, dated and signed by the testator with his own hand; it is subject to no other form.

The recognition given such an instrument as a valid testamentary instrument despite the lack of compliance with the formalities of attestation is attributed to the fact that a successful counterfeit of another's handwriting is exceedingly difficult and that the requirement that it be in the testator's handwriting would afford protection against forgery. Although written by the testator himself, a holographic will is a solemn act, and no matter how clearly it conveys the wishes of the decedent, it is not valid if it does not meet the statutory requirements. It is sufficient if the writing expresses, however informally, a testamentary purpose in language sufficiently clear to be understood.

Holographic wills are valid in 23 states. The state statutes governing holographic wills follow. They are paraphrased for each state.

- A will is valid as a holographic will if the signature and the material provisions are in the handwriting of the testator in the following states:

Alaska	13.11.160
Arizona	14–2503
Colorado	15–11–503
Idaho	15–2–503
Maine	18A–2–503
Michigan	27.5123
Montana	91A–2–503
Nebraska	30–2328
New Jersey	3B–3–3
North Dakota	30.1–08–03
Tennessee	32–105
Utah	75–2–503
Wyoming	2–6–113

- When the entire body of the will and the signature are in the handwriting of the testator, it may be established by the evidence of at least three disinterested witnesses to the handwriting and signature of the testator, without subscribing witnesses, in:

Arkansas	60–404

- A will written entirely in the testator's handwriting and signed and dated by him is valid in the following states:

California	Probate Code 53
Louisiana	C.C. 1588
Nevada	133.090
Oklahoma	84.54
South Dakota	29–2–8

- A holographic will is valid if it is wholly written and subscribed by the testator in the following states:

  Mississippi . . . .   91 – 5 – 1
  Virginia . . . .   64.1 – 49
  West Virginia . . . . . .   41 – 1 – 3

- A will wholly written by the testator is valid in:

  Texas . . . .   Probate Code 60

If you reside in any of these states, the holographic will might be adequate if you execute it in accordance with your own state statutes. It is anticipated that other states will recognize the holographic will in the future.

WHO MAY MAKE A WILL?

Your right to designate who will receive your property is dependent upon your possession of testamentary power and testamentary capacity. It is important to know and understand the distinction between the two. *Testamentary power* is the right by will to pass property to others of your choosing; that is, what property may be willed and to whom it may be given. *Testamentary capacity* is the mental competency to make a will. For the most part, if you have testamentary power and capacity, you may dispose of your property by will to such persons and for such purposes as you choose, provided, of course, that disposition is not contrary to some statute or common law rule.

The general power of testamentary disposition is founded on the assumption that a rational will is a better disposition than any that can be made by the law itself. Testamentary power involves a privilege under the law to make a will, while testamentary capacity concerns the ability of the testator to make a will. For example, at common law, convicts and married women had the capacity to make a will, but were denied the power to make a will by the old common law rules.

State statutes still require a person to be a certain age before he is considered competent to make a will. The statutes vary from age 14 to 19. I have no rational explanation as to why a 14-year-old person in Georgia can legally make a will disposing of real estate while across the border in Alabama, a person must be 18. It is, of course, obvious that many people under 21 years of age do not feel a strong need for a will; however, it is equally obvious that many people under that age of 21 might have an overriding need for executing a valid will. In all events, it is necessary to look to the specific statutes in each state to determine the legal age for making a will.

The age requirements of each of the states follow:

- Every person 18 years of age or older:

Alabama	Kentucky	Ohio
Arizona	Maine	Oklahoma
Arkansas	Maryland	Oregon
California	Massachusetts	Pennsylvania
Colorado	Michigan	Rhode Island
Connecticut	Minnesota	South Carolina
District of Columbia	Mississippi	South Dakota
Delaware	Missouri	Tennessee
Florida	Montana	Texas
Hawaii	Nebraska	Utah
Idaho	Nevada	Virginia
Illinois	New Hampshire	Washington
Indiana	New York	West Virginia
Iowa	North Carolina	Wisconsin
Kansas	North Dakota	

- Majority: New Mexico
- Full age: Vermont
- Every person 19 or more years of age: Alaska
- Every person except infants under 14: Georgia
- Legal age: Wyoming

HOW TO WRITE YOUR OWN WILL

As you have seen, the essential elements of a will are:

- A written instrument
- A competent testator
- An intent to dispose of property after death
- Execution of the will in accordance with statutory requirements

A will contains much more than these elements, and is limited only by the specific needs and desires of the person who writes it.

Although it is not absolutely essential to make a current inventory of your assets before you write your will, it is advisable to do so. The usual inventory includes such items as real estate, cash, automobiles, tangible personal property, stocks, bonds, insurance, profit sharing and pension funds, mutual funds, loans owed to you, business interests, and miscellaneous items. An essential part of estate planning consists of knowing the nature and extent of your current assets. In preparing your inventory of assets, you will find it much easier to make a decision as to what dispositions you wish to make in your will.

The Main Parts of a Will

Following is a checklist of the specific subjects usually found in a will. I will cover each of these subjects to the extent necessary to give you all the information you need to prepare a will. It will provide examples of specific language to accomplish your objectives as well as examples of typical wills that should cover all your needs. In drafting a will, you should use straightforward, commonly understood words and phrases that are not ambiguous or subject to misunderstandings. If a phrase, sentence, or paragraph is not clear in its meaning, it might be misinterpreted later. You should write simply, but strive to be precise and clear in stating your intentions. You should describe the specific results you want to accomplish. The more you know about wills and how the courts interpret them, the better prepared you will be to draft one of your own. The typical will usually contains the following parts:

- Introduction or Publication Clause
- Special Instructions
- Appointment of Executor, Executrix, Trustee, or Guardian
- General Gifts
- Specific Gifts
- Residuary Clause
- Execution of Will (Testimonium Clause)
- Attestation Clause
- Signatures and Addresses of Witnesses
- Self-Proof of Will

It is not mandatory that the contents be in any particular order, except that your signature and signatures of the witnesses should be located at the end of the instrument. Also, it is more convenient to have the appointment of the executor or executrix on the first page, especially if you have a long will. If your will is more than one page, it is good practice to sign in the margin on each page as well as on the last page. The signature at the end of the will is the only one that must be witnessed, however. Fasten the pages together securely. It is recommended that the material be spaced so that the closing parts of the will — the testimonium clause, signature, attestation clause, and the witnesses' signatures — appear on the same page. After you have studied this chapter carefully, you will be better able to select, from the forms at the end of the chapter, the language necessary for a draft of your own will.

The basic will forms provided at the end of this chapter are used by most of the people who write wills. In fact, unless your estate exceeds $600,000 or you have some special estate problem, one of these basic wills is preferred. With the use of these forms and the additional provisions, you should have no difficulty in drafting your will. If you are one of the few who has estate tax implications or other special situations, it is appropriate and proper for you to obtain professional assistance. If you decide to consult a professional, the knowledge you gain from reading this book will save you and your professional consultant a lot of time, which should cut down on the fees.

Introductory or Publication Clause

The Introductory Clause is the part that identifies the testator. It states that this is your last will and testament and that you are of sound mind and memory. It may be used to revoke all prior wills, if any. Following are the usual phrases used:

I, John Doe, of the City of _____, State of _____, being of sound and disposing mind and memory, do make, publish and declare this to be my Last Will and Testament, and hereby revoke all former wills and codicils by me made.

I, John Doe, being of sound and disposing mind and memory and hereby intending to dispose of all property belonging to me at my death, of whatever kind and wherever situation, do make, publish and declare this to be my Last Will and Testament.

Special Instructions

The law imposes a legal obligation to pay debts, and although it is not necessary to include a statement on the debts, such a statement is usually found in most wills. When a surviving spouse is obligated to pay the burial expenses of a deceased spouse, it can make a difference in the administration of the estate. This is a question you should discuss fully with your family when you are preparing your will.

It is unnecessary to give specific directions about burial, but this is another question you may wish to discuss with your family. Actually burial desires should be indicated through separate written instructions and not included as a part of your will. Because of the high costs associated with the typical "funeral," many people now give specific directions to avoid these expenses. Instructions for cremation and donation to research foundations seem to be the trend among people in this country. The usual provisions are:

My executor, hereinafter named, shall give my body a burial suitable to the wishes of my relatives and friends, and pay all of my funeral expenses, together with all my just debts, out of the first moneys coming into my estate.

I direct that I be interred in a plot owned by me in _____ cemetery in the City of _____, State of_____, more particularly known as _____ (Legal Description) _____, and that a suitable headstone be erected and inscribed upon said lot. The total cost of my funeral including the headstone shall be upwards of_____ Dollars, and for the purpose of providing for the perpetual care of said plot in said cemetery I hereby give, devise and bequeath to said cemetery, its successors and assigns the sum of _____ Dollars.

It is my wish and I direct that my body shall be cremated after my death.

Appointment of Executor, Executrix, Trustee, or Guardian

Who should you appoint as executor or executrix of your will? Who should be appointed guardian of minor children or trustee of any trust you establish? These are important questions and should receive careful consideration. The answers will depend entirely upon your own particular situation. The following general rules and suggestions will be helpful.

If you have a relatively small estate, you might wish to designate your spouse, a close relative, or a good friend to be the executor or executrix, the guardian of your children, or the trustee of your trusts. If there are no extensive business activities involved, no complicated real estate transactions, and no other major complications, these appointments are generally satisfactory and usually result in no difficulties and savings on administration expenses. If a relatively large estate is primarily liquid assets or assets that easily can be converted to liquid assets, such appointments are also satisfactory. Moreover, the more family members do in the probate of an estate, the more the savings of probate expenses and attorney's fees.

Where an estate has a substantial interest in an active business necessitating active participation, complex partnership interests, extensive real estate holdings, or other assets that require active management and participation, it might be a big mistake to appoint your wife, mother, sister, or friend. In this event, you should consider the appointment of a bank or trust company or a professional consultant who is qualified to handle such matters. If you appoint your wife, she probably would be required to employ someone to do the job (work) and would still be legally responsible as executrix of the estate. If you are involved in such a business, obtain advice from your banker, accountant, or attorney as to how you can find a well-qualified trust company or a professional to designate as the executor.

If you have minor children or close relatives who are minors and otherwise unable to handle their own business affairs, you may set up a trust and designate a trustee to administer the trust until the beneficiaries become adults. The same general principles apply to the appointment of a guardian as to an executor, with the exception that when possible and appropriate, it is usually preferable to have an adult relative appointed the guardian of very young children. You cannot always assume that the guardian of your minor children will be your surviving spouse. Simultaneous deaths are not uncommon. You should consider these questions carefully, and you might want to discuss them with your family. Your personal choice usually will be better than an appointment made by some judge who might not know you or your relatives.

After the selection for these appointments is made, you should select alternates as successors to these appointments. There is no assurance that the person you designate at first will be able to act, or that the designated person will survive you. You should also carefully consider whether to waive bond; this is generally recommended to save costs and expenses assuming, of course, that you have confidence in your appointees. Some suggested forms follow:

I hereby appoint Tom Doe of the City of _____ _____, State of _____, and the First National Bank of _____, executors of this my Last Will and Testament.

I hereby appoint Tom Doe of the City of _____ _____, State of _____, executor of this my Last Will and Testament, and direct that no bond or other undertaking be required of him for the faithful performance of the duties of his office.

I hereby nominate, constitute, and appoint my brother, Tom Doe, and the First National Bank and Trust Company of _____, as executors of this my Last Will and Testament. If my brother, Tom Doe, shall predecease me, then and in that event, I nominate, constitute, and appoint my cousin, Tim Doe, and the First National Bank and Trust Company of _____, as executors of this my Last Will and Testament. I hereby expressly direct that no bond or other security shall be required of said executors or either of them, in any jurisdiction, to secure the faithful performance of their respective duties as such.

(Guardian): I hereby appoint Mark Manning Guardian of the person and property of my children, Tom, Bob, and Mary, to serve during the minority of each, and I direct that no bond or other undertaking be required of him for the performance of the duties of such office, and in the event that said Mark Manning shall die or move his residence from the City of _____, or otherwise is un-

51

able to serve, then I revoke his appointment as such guardian and in his stead appoint John Jones guardian of the person and property of my said children during their minority, and I direct that no bond or other undertaking be required of him in the performance of the duties of such office.

General Gifts

General legacies are usually in money, but might be in other forms of personal property.

I give and bequeath to Mark Doe the sum of _____ Dollars.

I give and bequeath to Mark Doe fifty (50) shares of common stock of A.T.& T.

I give and bequeath to my trustee hereinafter named the sum of Fifty Thousand ($50,000) Dollars in cash, or the equivalent in value thereof in securities found in my estate, in trust, nevertheless, to collect and pay over the income arising therefrom to . . .

Specific Gifts

Specific gifts are of particular personal property which is specifically designated. For example, such items as jewelry, antiques, art objects, and other tangible objects are specific gifts.

I give and bequeath my white pearl pin to my son, Tom Doe.

I give and bequeath my Cadillac automobile License No. XLT-197 to my son, Tom Doe.

Residuary Clauses

The residuary clause can be a very important part of a will — or it can be of no significance. That is, if there is nothing left in the estate, it is of no significance. On the other hand, if a person should "strike it rich" just before demise, then the residuary clause would cover the disposition of all of the estate not specifically treated in the other provisions of the will. In the event a beneficiary of a specific bequest predeceases you, that property also would become a part of the residuary estate.

> All the rest, residue, and remainder of property, real personal, and mixed, at whatever time acquired by me and wheresoever situated, I give, devise, and bequeath to . . .

I give the residue of my estate to my wife Jane.

Execution of a Will

The courts do not have the power to add to or subtract from the statutory requirements that govern the signing of a will. As the testator, your intention in this regard is also of no importance. You must comply with the requirements of your state statute.

The written will must be signed in some way by you and, to be valid, must be witnessed by competent persons. The only allowable exceptions are the rather unusual procedures previously mentioned — holographic wills and nuncupative wills.

You may personally subscribe your name, make your mark, have another person write your name for you, or have another person guide your hand or affix your fingerprint. Practically any court will hold that the will is valid if you affix your mark instead of write your name. The signature by a third party is sufficient if made in your presence and at your direction, and if you assent to and adopt such signature as your own. If you are physically unable to sign your name, you may seek assistance from another person to help you write your name. As long as you participate in the act of signing your name and adopt it as your signature, the will is valid.

Frequent reference has been made to the signing of a will *in accordance with statutory requirements*. It is essential that you strictly comply with the requirements of any statute that governs the disposition of property. You should take precautions when signing your will to avoid the mistakes that have generated will contests in the past.

Here is a recommended procedure to follow in the execution and attestation of a will.

- Prepare the final draft of the will, preferably on a typewriter, with an original and one or more copies. Type the attestation clause in the proper place. Allow ample space for your signature and the signatures of the witnesses. Number the pages and bind them together firmly. Make certain that you thoroughly understand the meaning of every part of the will.

- Bring the witnesses together. Three witnesses will satisfy the requirements in all states except Louisiana. The witnesses should not be beneficiaries under the will or spouses of a beneficiary.
- Inform the witnesses that the document before them is your last will. It is not necessary or even desirable that they be allowed to read it. Then state that you are about to sign the will and request the witnesses to witness your signature.
- Then, with all the witnesses observing your action, sign the will. You should sign only the original; the carbon copies, as a matter of good practice, remain unsigned but conformed. After you sign the will, say to the witnesses, "This is my signature and this is my will. Will you please sign as attesting witnesses?"
- Next, have the witnesses read the attestation clause. Then have each witness sign immediately below the attestation clause and write his address. Neither you nor any of the witnesses should leave the room until all have signed the document. Each signature must be observed by you and all the other witnesses.

Now the document is a will. Place the signed original in a safe place where it is available to you and to the executor. Do not place it in a safe deposit vault because a court order might be required to get it out. The unsigned copies should be conformed through typing or writing in the information from the original. Place the copies in a different safe place.

Three witnesses are required by the statutory requirements of New Hampshire, South Carolina, and Vermont. All other states except Louisiana require two witnesses, except for the holographic will. As you have seen, the holographic will, which is legal in 23 states, needs no witnesses.

Most statutes require that the witnesses be competent or credible. A competent witness has been defined as a person who could, at the time of attesting to the will, legally testify in court to the facts to which he attests by subscribing his name to the will. *Credible* is ordinarily used in the same sense as *competent*.

Attestation Clause

Most states require only two witnesses to a will, but it is desirable to have at least three. Witnesses who are permanent residents of your city are preferable, and their addresses should always appear on the will.

The attestation clause is not, by legal definition, a part of the will. It follows the will and is the written and signed statement of the witnesses. Its use is strongly recommended because it is strong evidence that the will has been properly prepared. It serves as an authoritative memorandum to refresh the memories of the witnesses.

It is a good practice to include a statement that the will complies with all the statutory requirements. It is also recommended practice to state the number of pages in the will. If there have been any erasures or corrections in the will (and there should not be), they should be referred to in the attestation clause, making it clear that the erasures or corrections were made by you before you signed the will. Typical attestation clauses follow:

The foregoing instrument, consisting of three (3) typewritten pages, including this page, was signed, sealed, published, and declared by John Doe as his Last Will And Testament, in the presence of each of us, who at his request and in his presence and in the presence of one another, subscribe our names hereto as witnesses on the day of the date hereof; and we declare that at the time of the execution of this instrument the said John Doe, according to our best knowledge and belief, was of sound and disposing mind and memory and under no constraint.

Signed, sealed, published, and declared by John Doe, the above named testator, who appears to us to be of sound and disposing mind and memory, as and for his Last Will and Testament in our presence, and we, at his request, in his presence and in the presence of each other, have hereunto subscribed our names as witnesses this _____ day of _____, 19____.

Self-Proof of Will

A procedural device for the easy proof of wills has been enacted in most states. This procedure is recommended by the

Uniform Probate Code and probably will be adopted by all states in the future. It is a further modernization and simplification of the probate procedures in that it can be used as proof of a will without the need to call in witnesses to do so (unless the will is contested). The self-proof of a will may be made while the will is being written or subsequent to that time. As the testator, your acknowledgment of the will and the affidavits of the witnesses are made before an officer who is authorized to administer oaths. That person's authority is evidenced by the certificate attached to or following the will. This procedure is not required or necessary, but it is recommended that you use it if a notary public or other authorized official is available at the execution of the will. It might save a great deal of time, expense, and effort, and it adds to the formality of the will.

A suggested form of the Self-Proof acknowledgment is as follows:

State of _____
County of _____
We, _____(Name)_____, _____(Name)_____, _____(Name)_____, and _____(Name)_____, the testator and witnesses respectively, whose names are signed to the attached or foregoing instrument, were sworn and declared to the undersigned officer that the testator signed the instrument as his last will, that he signed, and that each of the witnesses, in the presence of the testator and in the presence of each other, signed the will as a witness.

_____(Signature)_____
Testator

_____(Signature)_____
_____(Signature)_____
_____(Signature)_____
Witnesses

Subscribed and sworn to before me by _____(Name)_____, the testator, and by _____(Name)_____, _____(Name)_____, and _____(Name)_____, the witnesses on the _____ day of _____, 19_____.

_____(Signature)_____
Official Capacity of Officer

An *acknowledgment* is a public declaration or formal statement of the person executing an instrument that is made to the office authorized to take the acknowledgment and that states the execution of the instrument was his free act and deed. It is written evidence of an acknowledgment and generally states that the person named in the document was known to the official, appeared before him, and acknowledged the instrument to be his act and deed. An *affidavit* is a written statement made voluntarily and sworn to or affirmed before a person legally authorized to administer an oath or affirmation. Generally, any person who has knowledge of the facts sworn to in the writing may make an affidavit.

As a general rule, officers authorized to take acknowledgments include judges, clerks of court, notaries public, commissioners, and justices of the peace. Each state has a statute that make these designations. In foreign countries, the authorized officials usually include judges of a court of record, diplomatic counselors or commercial agents of the United States, and notaries public. Certain designated military personnel have authority to administer oaths for purposes of military administration, including military justice, and to act as notary and United States Consul in the performance of all notarial acts to be executed by members of the armed forces.

Miscellaneous Clauses

There are a number of other items that might be appropriate in a will. Some of these follow.

Forgiveness of Debts. If you wish to forgive a specific debt owed to you by a person whom you designate as a beneficiary under your will, make a specific statement in the will of this intention. If you intend for the debt to be deducted from the legacy, state such an intent in the will.

I give and bequeath to Mark Manning the sum of Five Thousand ($5,000) Dollars. I release and discharge said Mark Manning of any and all outstanding debts and interest thereon due me from him at the time of my death, and direct that the said Five Thousand ($5,000) Dollars be paid to the said Mark Manning in full, without any deduction on account of such indebtedness.

Forfeiture of Legacy of One Who Contests Will. These clauses are not enforceable in some circumstances in a few states. They are not favored by some courts, and you should not rely on them too heavily.

Any beneficiary under this my will who shall institute, prosecute, or abet any action to contest or to set aside in whole or in part this my will shall be excluded from any share or interest in my estate as legatee, devisee, heir at law, next of kin or otherwise, and I hereby direct that the property or interest to which he or she might otherwise have become entitled shall form and become a part of my residuary estate.

If any objection shall be made to the probate of this will or any attempt shall be made to revoke the probate thereof by any of my heirs, next of kin, legatees, devisees, or any beneficiary under any provision of this will, or in case any contest shall arise as to the carrying into effect of any article thereof, it is my will that any heir, next of kin, legatee, devisee, or beneficiary under any provision of this will who shall make or offer or permit to be made or offered any such objection or attempt or who shall inaugurate or raise or abet any such contest shall be reason thereof forfeit any and all right or interest which he or she might otherwise have under this my will, or in my estate, and shall be excluded from any share or interest in my estate as legatee, devisee, heir at law, next of kin, or otherwise, and I hereby give, devise, and bequeath the property, interest, articles, or money constituting such devise, legacy, or share in my estate to which he or she or they might otherwise become entitled to such of my residuary legatees as shall not have violated this provision of my will.

Common Disaster Clause or Simultaneous Death Clause. It is depressing enough to contemplate your own death, but you should also consider the remote possibility of common disasters. Common disasters or simultaneous deaths are unfortunate, but it is equally unfortunate to see an estate shrink in size by being "probated" two or three times within a few years. It is one of the primary objectives of a good will to avoid unnecessary taxes and administrations expenses. Here are examples of these clauses.

In the event that any beneficiary under this my will and I shall die under circumstances that there is no sufficient evidence that we died otherwise than simultaneously, such beneficiary shall be deemed to have predecreased me.

In the event my said wife shall predecease me or shall die simultaneously with me, or so nearly so that it cannot be determined which of us survived the other, then in either such events I give, devise, and bequeath all of the rest, residue, and remainder of my property and estate described in the preceding Article _____, hereof, absolutely and in fee simple, unto the First National Bank and Trust Co. of _____, as Trustee, to hold the same with full discretionary powers of managements, sale and resale, investment and reinvestment and to keep the same invested, in trust, however, for the following uses and purposes, namely . . .

Upon condition that my wife die prior to the date six months subsequent to my death, but only that condition and not otherwise, I hereby give, devise, and bequeath all of my estate, of every kind and nature, both real and personal and wheresoever situated to my lawful descendants, equally, share and share alike.

Codicil. A *codicil* is an instrument that either adds to or changes an existing will. A codicil, to be valid, must meet all the statutory requirements of a will. In most instances, a codicil is merely a temporary change of a will until the testator has time to rewrite the entire will. Significant or extensive changes usually should not be made by codicil. It is recommended that you prepare a new will instead of relying upon codicils unless there is some compelling reason not to rewrite the will. For example, if a person is nearing senility or incapacity, it is not recommended that he write a new will, but make a codicil for any changes. With the knowledge and information you have learned in this book, it will be as easy to write a new will as to write a codicil.

Revocation of Wills. To *revoke* a will means to annul it in whole or in part. A revocation may be expressed by virtue of a revocation clause contained in a later will, or implied by reason of an inconsistent disposition of property in a later will. Under some statutes, a change in the circumstances of the testator subsequent to the execution of the will might constitute a revocation by operation of law. Therefore, it is important to review your will periodically, or after any significant change in your circumstances, to assure yourself that your will meets with your desires and intention. Upon being revoked, a testamentary provision ceases to exist, and is inoperative. It is as if it had never been written.

A will may be revoked by tearing it up, cutting, burning, cancelling, erasing, obliterating, and any other physical act that essentially destroys the will, so long as the acts are intended by you, the testator, as a revocation. A will also might be revoked by operation of law, or as it is sometimes called, *revocation implied by law*. Such a revocation might result from certain circumstances not specifically mentioned in the statutes that prescribe the proper methods of revocation. The doctrine is that the revocation of a will can be implied by certain changes in your family, domestic relations, your property, or one of the beneficiaries of your will. By these actions, the law infers or presumes that you intended to change the will. The intended change might be either total or partial. The rule is based on the theory that, by reason of such changes subsequent to the date of the will, you have acquired new moral duties and obligations. Subsequent marriage or divorce might have a significant change in the will. The death of the sole beneficiary in effect abrogates the will. Changes in the character of the estate will change the effect of a will. The birth of additional children could have an effect on an existing will.

Although most people rarely revoke a will without immediately preparing another, it is important for you to be familiar with the changes imposed by law so you will be in a position to prepare your own will and change it from time to time to meet your special needs.

The final step in drafting a will is to assemble all of the facts and information about your estate, family, and personal situation. This is very important because it clearly defines your personal situation and enables you to crystallize your thinking about your estate and make a decision as to who you wish to have your assets. As discussed in Chapters 2 and 3, you also should give serious consideration to the concept that you might wish to avoid probate for all, or part, of your estate.

WILL FORMS AND ALTERNATIVE WILL PROVISIONS

In the earlier editions of my books on will writing, I sought to achieve simplicity in will writing; however, out of an abundance of caution — typical of lawyers — I included a wide variety of separate will forms. Many of my readers and friends have suggested that so many forms seemed to complicate the will-writing process. I agree. As a result of much research, study, discussion, meditation, and analysis, I have adopted a few basic will forms as guides to your will writing. I have eliminated the "marital deduction" clauses since we are working with estates that are exempt from federal estate taxes. There are two basic groups of people: those who have minor children, and those who do not. Thus, these basic will forms are adequate for a great majority of us. If you have tax problems or other legal entanglements, you will wish to seek professional advice; otherwise, the following forms should be adequate for most purposes.

After you have prepared an inventory of your estate and made a decision as to the specific objectives you wish to accomplish in your will, you can use one of the basic will forms, along with the optional will provisions, to prepare a proper will.

FORM 1: ENTIRE ESTATE TO PARENTS

LAST WILL AND TESTAMENT
OF
_____
(Name)

I, _____ *(Name)* _____, a resident of
_____ *(City)* _____, _____ *(State)* _____,
hereby make this Will, and revoke all prior Wills.

1. I direct that my debts and funeral expenses be paid by
my Executor/Executrix as soon as practicable after my death.

2. I give my entire estate to my mother,
_____ *(Name)* _____, or, if she predeceases me, then
to my father, _____ *(Name)* _____.

2. I hereby nominate and appoint,
_____ *(Name)* _____, Executor/Executrix of this Will.
I direct that no bond or other security shall be required of my
Executor/Executrix for the faithful performance of his/her
duties.

In Witness Whereof I have subscribed and sealed and do
publish and declare these presents as and for my Will in the
presence of the witnesses attesting the same this _____ day
of _____, 19_____.

_____ *(Signature)* _____
(Name)

(Attestation, Witnesses, Self-Proof, etc.)

62

FORM 2: ENTIRE ESTATE TO BENEFICIARY OR ALTERNATIVELY TO SECOND BENEFICIARY

LAST WILL AND TESTAMENT
OF
_____*(Name)*_____

I, _____*(Name)*_____ ,
of_____*(County)*_____ ,
_____*(State)*_____ , make this my last will, and
revoke all prior wills or codicils.

1. I direct that all my legal debts and funeral expenses be
paid as soon as practicable after my death.

2. I give my entire estate to _____*(Name)*_____
if she/he survives me. If she/he does not survive me, then I
give my estate to _____*(Name)*_____ .

3. I appoint _____*(Name)*_____ Executor/
Executrix hereunder and if she/he shall fail to qualify, or
having qualified, shall die, resign, or cease to act as
Executor/Executrix, then I appoint
_____*(Name)*_____ to act hereunder. No Executor/
Executrix named herein shall be required to give bond.

4. If any beneficiary and I should die in a common
accident or disaster, or under such circumstances that it is
doubtful who died first, or if any beneficiary dies within 30
[60, 90, 180] days of my death, then all the provisions of this
will shall take effect as if such beneficiary had in fact
predeceased me.

In Witness Whereof I have hereunto set my hand this
_____ day of _____, 19____ .

_____*(Signature)*_____
_____*(Name)*_____

(Attestation, Witnesses, Self-Proof, etc.)

FORM 3: ESTATE TO SPOUSE OR ALTERNATIVELY TO MINOR CHILDREN

LAST WILL AND TESTAMENT
OF
_____
(Name)

I, _____*(Name)*_____ , of
_____*(County)*_____ , _____*(State)*_____ ,
make this my last will, and revoke all prior wills or codicils.

1. I direct that all my legal debts and funeral expenses be paid as soon as practicable after my death.

2. I give my entire estate to my wife/husband, _____*(Name)*_____ , if she/he survives me. If _____*(Name)*_____ does not survive me, then I give my estate to my children _____*(Names)*_____ , share and share alike.

3. I appoint _____*(Name)*_____ Executor/ Executrix hereunder and if she/he shall fail to quality, or having qualified, shall die, resign, or cease to act as Executor/Executrix, then I appoint _____*(Name)*_____ to act hereunder. No Executor/ Executrix named herein shall be required to give bond.

4. If any beneficiary and I should die on a common accident or disaster, or under such circumstances that it is doubtful who dies first, or if any beneficiary dies with 30 [60, 90, 180] days of my death, then all the provisions of this will shall take effect as if such beneficiary had in fact predeceased me.

5. The share of any beneficiary who shall be under the age of 18 years shall not be paid to such beneficiary but shall instead be held in trust to apply to his/her use all the income thereof, and also such amounts of the principal, even to the extent of all, as my Trustee deems necessary or suitable for the support, welfare, and education of such beneficiary; and when he/she attains the age of 18 [21, 25] years to pay him/her the remaining principal, if any. If any beneficiary for whom a share is held in trust should die before having received all the principal thereof, then upon his/her death the remaining principal shall be paid to his/her then living child or children, equally if more than one, and in default thereof, to my then living descendants, per stirpes [of per capita].

6. If it shall be necessary to appoint a guardian for any minor child of mine, I appoint _____*(Name)*_____ as such guardian. If _____*(Name)*_____ shall fail to qualify, or having qualified, shall die, resign, or cease to act as such guardian, then I appoint _____*(Name)*_____ to serve as such guardian.

7. In the event any trust shall come into existence under this will, I appoint _____*(Name)*_____ as Trustee hereunder to serve without bond. If _____*(Name)*_____ shall fail to qualify, or having qualified, shall die, resign, or cease to act for any reason, I appoint _____*(Name)*_____ in his place and stead, to serve without bond.

In Witness Whereof I have hereunto set my hand this _____ day of _____, 19_____.

_____ *(Signature*

(Name)

(Attestation, Witnesses, Self-Proof, etc.)

FORM 4: HOLOGRAPHIC WILL (HANDWRITTEN)

LAST WILL OF _____ *(Name)* _____

This is my will, and I revoke all prior wills. I give all my property to my husband, _____ *(Name)* _____ , if he survives me, and if he predeceases me, then I give my property to my children, share and share alike.

I appoint my husband, _____ *(Name)* _____ , Executor of this will and waive all bonds. This will is written, dated, and signed by me in my own handwriting.

Dated this _____ day of _____, 19_____.

_____ *(Signature)* _____

OPTIONAL WILL PROVISIONS

General Gifts

I give and bequeath the sum of _____(Amount)_____ to my son, _____(Name)_____, if he shall survive me.

I give and bequeath the sum of _____(Amount)_____ to my daughter, _____(Name)_____, if she shall survive me.

I give to my father, _____(Name)_____, if he survives me, the sum of $50,000.

I give to the Red Cross for its general purposes, the sum of $50,000.

I give the sum of five thousand dollars ($5,000) to my friend, _____(Name)_____ if he/she survives me.

Specific Gifts

I give, devise, and bequeath to my wife, _____(Name)_____, if she survives me, in fee simple, the buildings and land located at _____(Street Address)_____, City of _____, State of _____. If my wife does not survive me, this gift shall lapse and the property described herein shall fall into and become part of my residuary estate.

I give and devise to my wife, _____(Name)_____, if she survives me, or if not, in equal shares to my children who survive me, their heirs and assigns forever, all real estate owned by me at the time of my death, including all buildings and improvements thereon, and all rights and other interests pertaining thereto.

I give and devise to my son, _____(Name)_____, and my daughter, _____(Name)_____, share and share alike, per stirpes and not per capita, the real property owned by me at _____(Street Address)_____, County of _____, State of _____, and further described as follows:_____.

Specific Legacies

I give and bequeath to my wife, _____(Name)_____, if she survives me, all my furniture, furnishings, books, linens, silver, china, glassware, jewelry, wearing apparel, automobiles, and other household and personal goods and effects.

To my daughter, _____(Name)_____, I give my diamond ring and my gold watch. If my daughter does not survive me, this legacy shall lapse and become part of my residuary estate.

I give and bequeath all my law books, office equipment, and all property contained in my law office to my son, _____(Name)_____, if he shall survive me.

General Legacies

I give and bequeath the sum of _____(Amount)_____ to _____(Name)_____ if he/she survives me, or if he/she does not, then per stirpes to those of his/her issue who survive him/her.

I give and bequeath the sum of _____(Amount)_____ to my friend, _____(Name)_____, if he/she survives me.

Dispositive Provisions

I give, devise, and bequeath my entire estate to my mother, _____(Name)_____, or if she predeceases me, then to my mother, _____(Name)_____.

I give my entire estate to my wife, _____(Name)_____, if she survives me.

If my wife, _____(Name)_____, does not survive me, I give my estate, in equal shares to my three children _____(Name)_____, _____(Name)_____, and _____(Name)_____. The share of any legatee who shall be under the age of 18 [21, 25] years shall not be paid to such legatee, but shall instead be held in trust to apply to his/her use all the income thereof, and also such amounts of the principal, even to the extent of all, as my Trustee deems necessary or suitable for the support, welfare, and education of such legatee; and when he/she attains the age of 18 [21, 25] years to pay him/her the remaining principal, if any. If any legatee for whom a share is held in trust should die before having received all the principal thereof, then upon his/her death the remaining principal shall be paid to his/her then living child or children, equally if more than one, and in default thereof, to my then living descendants, per stirpes [or per capita].

I give my entire estate equally to my surviving issue, per stirpes.

I give, devise, and bequeath all of my estate, of whatever kind and description and wherever situated to my wife, _____ *(Name)* _____, providing she shall survive me by 30 [60, 80] days.

If my wife, _____ *(Name)* _____, shall not survive me by 30 [60, 80] days, then I direct my Executor to divide my residuary estate into two equal parts, and to dispose of the same as follows:

I give the residue of my estate to my wife, _____ *(Name)* _____, or, if she does not survive me, to my surviving issue per stirpes.

General Bequest of Items of Personal Property

I give and bequeath to _____ *(Name)* _____ all of my household furniture, rugs, paintings, works of art, ornaments, tapestry, silverware, plate, books, linen, china, glassware, and all other household goods and supplies that I own at the time of my death.

It is my will and desire that _____ *(Name)* _____ shall have the benefit of four (4) years of college education, and I direct that my trustee pay from my estate all expenses of attendance for four (4) years at a recognized college, said expenses not to exceed the amount of _____ Dollars.

Bequest of Unpublished Manuscripts

I give and bequeath to _____ (Name) _____ all letters, papers, manuscripts, diaries, and other writings. This bequest, however, does not include legal documents, such as agreements, contracts, deeds, notes, or mortgages.

Devise of Family Home

If I own a house and plot of ground at the time of my death, which is being used by my wife and me as a family home, then I give, devise, and bequeath such house and plot of ground unto my said wife, subject, however, to any encumbrance or encumbrances thereon existing at the time of my death [or free and clear of any encumbrance thereon existing at the time of my death].

Personal Property

I give and bequeath all my household furnishings, furniture, jewelry, silverware, books, automobiles, wearing apparel, and all other personal effects which may be owned by me at the time of my death, together with all policies of insurance relating thereto, to my wife, _____ (Name) _____, if she survives me.

Bequest of Business

I give and bequeath the goodwill and benefit of the business of _____ (Name) _____, which I am now carrying on at _____ (Location) _____, and also all my capital and property which shall be employed therein at my decease and also the leasehold premises situated at _____ (Location) _____, wherein said business is now being carried on, for all my term and interest therein, unto my son, _____ (Name) _____, absolutely.

Gift of Automobiles and Furniture

I give to my wife, _____ (Name) _____, all my automobiles and household furniture and effects, together with any and all insurance policies thereon.

Gifts of Personal Effects and Household Goods

All my jewelry, clothing, personal effects, books, paintings, works of art, and all household goods and household furnishings of every description I give to _____ (Name) _____.

Appointment of Executor/Executrix

I constitute and appoint _____ *(Name)* _____ Executor of this will, and direct that no bond shall be required of any Executor or Executrix.

I appoint my wife, _____ *(Name)* _____, Executrix of this my last will and testament, or, if she predeceases me or fails to qualify as Executrix, I appoint my son, _____ *(Name)* _____, Substitute Executor. Neither shall be required to give any bond or other security for the faithful performance of their duties.

I appoint my wife, _____ *(Name)* _____, Executrix of this will. If my wife shall fail to qualify or cease to act, I appoint my brother, _____ *(Name)* _____, Executor in her place and stead. I appoint my brother, _____ *(Name)* _____, Trustee of the trusts hereunder. If my brother shall fail to qualify or cease to act in any of the foregoing capacities, I appoint my wife's sister, _____ *(Name)* _____, in such capacity in the place and stead of my brother. I direct that none of these individuals shall be required to file a bond or other security in any jurisdiction for the faithful performance of his/her duties.

Disinheritance of Heirs Not Named

I have intentionally omitted all my heirs who are not specifically mentioned herein, and I hereby generally and specifically disinherit each, any, and all persons whosoever claiming to be or who may be lawfully determined to be my heirs at law, except as otherwise mentioned in this will.

Omission of Any Person Except Spouse

I have intentionally omitted to mention, or to give anything to any person or persons other than my wife, _____ *(Name)* _____.

Bequest to Surviving Children

I give to my children who shall be living at the time of my death my entire estate, equally to be divided between them; and if any dispute should arise with respect to the division, I authorize my Executor to distribute the effects equally among my children.

Chapter 6

The Durable Power of Attorney

A *power of attorney* is an instrument in writing by which one person, as principal, appoints another as agent and confers upon the agent the authority to perform certain specified acts or kinds of acts on behalf of the principal. The written authorization itself is the power of attorney, and is sometimes referred to as a *letter of attorney*.

The main reason for having a power of attorney is not to define the relationship between the agent and the principal, but to evidence the authority of the agent to third parties with whom the agent deals. The person who acts under a power of attorney is called an *attorney in fact*, and this is not necessarily an attorney-client relationship. The term *attorney in fact* is defined by the law dictionary as:

A private attorney authorized by another to act in his place and stead, either for some particular purpose, as to do a particular act, or for the transaction of business in general, not of a legal character. This authority is conferred by an instrument in writing, called a "letter of attorney," or more commonly a "power of attorney."[1]

There are several kinds of power of attorney:

---

[1] *Black's Law Dictionary*, Fifth Ed.: 118

- The general power of attorney to transact business in general
- The specific power of attorney, which is limited to a specified act or kinds of acts
- The durable power of attorney (either general or specific), which expressly extends beyond the incapacity or disability of the principal

Most people think of estate planning as preparing for what happens after death—wills, probate, avoiding probate, etc. Did you know, however, that a 22-year-old person is $7\frac{1}{2}$ times more likely to suffer a disability lasting 90 days or more than he is to die? A 62-year-old person is $4\frac{1}{2}$ times more likely to suffer a disability lasting 90 days or more than to die. Have you ever thought about this possibility in connection with your estate planning? These statistics clearly show that although disability, unlike death, is not a certainty, it is far more likely to occur for persons under 60 than is death. The problem of disability, therefore, requires serious consideration in your estate planning. If you overlook this apparently remote occurrence, your entire estate plans might collapse.

A durable power of attorney, an essential part of all good estate planning, can solve this problem. It enables your agent to handle business and personal matters even if you are unable to do so.

A power of attorney is an agency relationship between a principal and agent, and until recently was governed by common law principles of agency, which meant that an *agency* relationship was automatically terminated by the death or incompetency of the principal. Many states have now enacted some version of the Durable Power of Attorney Act, as recommended by the National Conference of Commissioners on Uniform State Laws. This statute provides that a properly executed durable power of attorney is not to terminate upon the incapacity or disability of the principal. The Durable Power of Attorney Act generally requires a provision in the power of attorney that *This power of attorney shall not be affected by subsequent disability or incapacity of the principal,* or *This power of attorney shall become effective upon the disability or incapacity of the principal,* or similar words showing the intent of the principal that the authority conferred shall be exercisable notwithstanding the principal's subsequent disability or incapacity.

This definition, based upon the Uniform Act, reflects the efforts of the National Conference of Commissioners on Uniform State Laws to formulate a uniform statement of the law as it should be. The durable power of attorney provision is a part of the Uniform Probate Code, which has been adopted in many states. Therefore, you should have no difficulty in ascertaining the status of your state laws on this issue. A durable power of attorney should be effective in some situations even in the absence of a specific statutory enactment of the Uniform Act.

In addition to the recent enactment of this statute in many states, there is a general principle of law that the incapacity of a principal does not necessarily make a general power of attorney void (in the absence of a judicial determination of incapacity), but only voidable. Therefore, it is generally held by some authorities that a general power of attorney is not terminated until, and unless, a court of competent jurisdiction makes a finding, determination, and adjudication of incapacity. Thus, a properly executed durable power of attorney is considered to be an effective estate-planning technique in all states, if it is properly prepared and if the agent and principal know how to handle the practical application of the transactions.

The old rule of law that a power of attorney should terminate upon incapacity of the principal has not been seen as a very practical result. Indeed, one judge said:

> Men who enter hospitals for major surgery often execute powers of attorney to enable others to continue their business affairs during their incapacity. Any judicial doctrine which would legally terminate such power as of the inception of the incapacity would be startling indeed — it would disrupt commercial affairs and entirely without reason or purpose.

It is, therefore, recommended that you consider the durable power of attorney as a part of your estate planning.

GENERAL PRINCIPLES OF AGENCY LAW

The power of attorney is essentially an agency relationship. It is controlled by principles of agency law as modified by statutes. You should not be confused by the title *attorney in fact*. This term does not necessarily mean an attorney at law; it is merely the designation of the agent who is authorized to act for you. An *agency* is a fiduciary relationship by which one party confides to another the management of some business to be transacted in the first party's name or on his account, and by which the second party assumes to do the business and render an account of it. It is a relationship in which one person acts as agent for a principal pursuant to the authority of the principal. The law dictionary defines agency as:

> The relation created by express or implied contract or by law, whereby one party delegates the transaction of some lawful business with more or less discretionary power of another, who undertakes to manage the affair and render to him an account thereof. Agency is the fiduciary relation which results from the manifestation of consent by one person to another that the other shall act on his behalf and subject to his control, and consent by the other so to act.[2]

THE DURABLE POWER OF ATTORNEY

The word *durable* is defined as:

> . . . lasting or enduring; holding out well against wear or any destructive change, able to continue long in the same state, having the quality of enduring, having power to resist decay, impervious to change, not easily worn out, enduring, persisting, permanent, abiding, lasting, constant, perpetual, everlasting . . .

STATUTORY PROVISIONS

The provisions of the Uniform Probate Code governing the durable power of attorney are as follows:

Sec 5-501. Definition.
    A durable power of attorney is a power of attorney by which a principal designates another his attorney in fact in writing and the writing contains the words "This power of attorney shall not be affected by subsequent disability or incapacity of the principal," or "This power of attorney shall become effective upon the disability or incapacity of the

---

[2]Ibid: 57,58

principal," or similar words showing the intent of the principal that the authority conferred shall be exercisable notwithstanding the principal's subsequent disability or incapacity.

Sec 5-502. Durable Power of Attorney Not Affected by Disability or Incapacity.

All acts done by an attorney in fact pursuant to a durable power of attorney during any period of disability or incapacity of the principal have the same effect and inure to the benefit of and bind the principal and his successors in interest as if the principal were competent and not disabled.

The Uniform Act defined *incapacitated person* as

any person who is impaired by reason of mental illness, mental deficiency, physical illness or disability, advanced age, chronic use of drugs, chronic intoxication, or other cause (except minority) to the extent of lacking sufficient understanding or capacity to make or communicate responsible decisions.[3]

No matter how well you plan your estate, plan for the probate of your estate, or plan for avoiding probate, you will not have completed your estate planning well without addressing the serious problem of handling your estate in the event of your disability or incapacity. The statistics on disability tell an awesome tale. The appointment of an attorney in fact is easy to accomplish, and it has the potential for avoiding tragic consequences. I hope you never need it, but be prepared.

The following forms are for your use in completing your own Durable Power of Attorney. These two forms contain the "durable" provision. In the event you wish to prepare a power of attorney that is not "durable," you simply eliminate the sentence, *This power of attorney shall not be affected by subsequent disability or incapacity of the principal.*

---

[3]U.P.C., Sec. 1-201(7)

FORM 5: DURABLE POWER OF ATTORNEY: GENERAL POWERS

STATE OF _____

COUNTY OF _____

KNOW ALL MEN BY THESE PRESENTS, THAT I

_____ *(Name)* _____ , as Principal, of

_____ *(Address)* _____ , constitute, and

appoint _____ *(Name)* _____ , of

_____ *(Address)* _____ , City of

_____ , State of

_____ , as my true and lawful attorney in
fact for me and in my name, place, and stead, giving unto my
said attorney in fact full power to do and perform all and
every act, deed, matter, and thing whatsoever in and about
my estate, property, and affairs as fully and effectually to all
intents and purposes as I might or could do in my own proper
person, if personally present, with full power of substitution
and revocation, hereby ratifying and affirming that which my
named attorney in fact shall lawfully do or cause to be done
by virtue of the power herein conferred upon him/her. This
power of attorney shall not be affected by my subsequent
disability or incapacity.

_____ *(Signature)* _____

Principal

                 _____ *(Signature)* _____

                 Witness

                 _____ *(Signature)* _____

                 Witness

                 _____ *(Signature)* _____

                 Witness

Attestation and Acknowledgment

We, _____ *(Names)* _____ , as Principal, and

_____ *(Name)* _____ , _____ *(Name)* _____ ,

and _____ *(Name)* _____ the witnesses respectively,
were sworn and declared to the undersigned officer that the
Principal signed the instrument as his/her Durable Power of
Attorney, that he/she signed, and that each of the witnesses,
in the presence of the Principal and in the presence of each
other, signed the instrument as witnesses, and we declare at
the time of the execution of this instrument the Principal, to

our best knowledge and belief, was of sound and disposing mind and memory and under no constraint.

_____*(Signature)*_____
Principal

                          _____*(Signature)*_____
                          Witness
                          _____*(Signature)*_____
                          Witness
                          _____*(Signature)*_____
                          Witness

Sworn to and subscribed before me this _____ day of _____, 19____.
My Commission Expires:

_____*(Date)*_____   _____*(Signature)*_____
                          Notary Public

FORM 6: DURABLE POWER OF ATTORNEY—
specific powers

Durable Power of Attorney

STATE OF _____
COUNTY OF _____
KNOW ALL MEN BY THESE PRESENTS, THAT I,
_____ , as Principal, of
       (Name)
_____ , City of
       (Address)
_____ , State of
_____ , hereby make, constitute, and
appoint _____ , of
              (Name)
_____ , City of
       (Address)
_____ , State of
_____ , as my true and lawful attorney in
fact for me and in my name, place, and stead, to do the
following act or acts:_____
_____
_____ ,

hereby ratifying and affirming that which my named attorney
in fact shall lawfully do or cause to be done by virtue of the
power herein conferred upon him/her. This power of attorney
shall not be affected by my subsequent disability or incapacity.

_____
       (Signature)
Principal
                         _____
                                (Signature)
                         Witness
                         _____
                                (Signature)
                         Witness
                         _____
                                (Signature)
                         Witness

Attestation and Acknowledgment
We, _____ , as Principal, and
              (Name)
_____ , _____ ,
       (Name)   *(Name)*
and _____ , the witnesses respectively,
              (Name)
were sworn and declared to the undersigned officer that the
Principal signed the instrument as his/her Durable Power of
Attorney, that he/she signed, and that each of the witnesses,
in the presence of the Principal and in the presence of each
other, signed the instrument as witnesses, and we declare at

the time of the execution of this instrument the Principal, to our best knowledge and belief, was of sound and disposing mind and memory and under no constraint.

_____*(Signature)*_____
Principal

_____*(Signature)*_____
Witness

_____*(Signature)*_____
Witness

_____*(Signature)*_____
Witness

Sworn to and subscribed before me this_____ day of
_____, 19_____.

My Commission Expires:

_____*(Date)*_____ _____*(Signature)*_____
Notary Public

Finally, the Supreme Court declared that a nonmarital partner may recover in quantum meruit for the reasonable value of household services less the reasonable value of support received. The action was remanded to the Superior Court where evidence has been taken in implementation of the above described decision. The last mentioned remedy, quantum meruit, need not be considered here inasmuch as the plaintiff has dismissed her fourth and fifth causes of action based on such ground.

The first three causes of action, amended to reflect the remedies described by the Supreme Court, allege contractual, express and implied and equitable bases for judgment in favor of plaintiff.

In order to comply with the Supreme Court mandate, the trial court collected all available evidence which might bear on the relationship established after defendant allegedly promised plaintiff half of his property or which might serve as a basis for a tacit agreement or for equitable relief.

After the trial of the case in the trial court, the judge found from the evidence that there was no express contract, there was no implied contract, and there was no fact situation giving rise to a constructive trust or resulting trust. However, the trial judge said:

In view of these circumstances, the court in equity awards plaintiff $104,000 for rehabilitation purposes so that she may have the economic means to reeducate herself and to learn new, employable skills or to refurbish those utilized, for example, during her most recent employment and so that she may return from her status as companion of a motion picture star to a separate, independent but perhaps more prosaic existence.[2]

In the Hewitt case, the Supreme Court of Illinois found several reasons why the Marvin decision was not persuasive in Illinois. The court then said:

[2]Marvin v. Marvin, Memorandum Opinion of Judge Arthur K. Marshall, Superior Court of The State of California for the County of Los Angeles.

Further, in enacting the Illinois Marriage and Dissolution of Marriage Act, our legislature considered and rejected the "no-fault" divorce concept that has been adopted in many other jurisdictions, including California . . . Illinois appears to be one of three States retaining fault grounds for dissolution of marriage.

We accordingly hold that plaintiff's claims are unenforceable for the reason that they contravene the public policy, implicit in the statutory scheme of the Illinois Marriage and Dissolution of Marriage Act, disfavoring the grant of mutually enforceable property rights to knowingly unmarried cohabitants. The judgment of the appellate court is reversed and the judgment of the circuit court of Champaign County is affirmed.[3]

[3] Hewitt v. Hewitt, 394 N.E. 2d 1211.

Chapter 8

Antenuptial Agreements

An *antenuptial agreement* is a contract between a man and a woman before marriage, but in contemplation and generally in consideration of marriage, whereby the property rights and interests of either the prospective husband or wife, or both of them, are determined, or where property is secured to either or both of them, or to their children.

As a general rule, certain aspects of these agreements have been sanctioned by the courts where the prospective marital partners contract to vary, limit, or relinquish certain rights which they would otherwise acquire in each other's property or in each other's estate by reason of their impending marriage. Where the agreement includes any antenuptial contingency planning in case of a later divorce or marital separation, however, the courts have until very recently held these provisions to be illegal and void, as against public policy. In practice, antenuptial agreements have traditionally been between older people who are about to be remarried and who have acquired considerable property from a prior marriage that they wish to control.

Thus, the courts sanction the basic principle of agreements about property rights, but have invalidated those provisions that facilitate, promote, or encourage a divorce or separation. The courts have held that these provisions are void as contrary to a rigid public policy rule, purportedly upholding the status of marriage by preventing the parties from executing a private agreement that would facilitate a future divorce or legal separation. One court stated the old rule as follows:

> . . . any antenuptial contract which provides for, facilitates, or tends to induce a separation or divorce of the parties after marriage is contrary to public policy, and is therefore void. It has often been held that an antenuptial agreement limiting the liability of the husband to the wife (or vice versa) for alimony, or fixing the property rights of the parties in the event of a separation or divorce, is void.[1]

The concept of marriage as a social institution that is the foundation of the family and of society remains unchanged. Because marriage is of vital interest to society and the state, it frequently has been said that in every divorce suit the state is a third party, whose interests take precedence over the private interests of the marital partners.

It is this same public policy that is the basis for the rule that an antenuptial agreement by which a prospective wife waives or limits her right to alimony or to the property of her husband in the event of divorce or separation, regardless of who is at fault, has been held invalid.

The legal rationale behind this public policy rule rests upon two premises:

- Antenuptial agreements that include provisions related to the possibility of divorce tend to promote or encourage that divorce.
- Certain duties incident to marriage, such as alimony or spousal support and maintenance, are of such public importance that they cannot be left to the parties' private contractual control in an antenuptial agreement.

The reasons for the rule are summarized as follows:

> An antenuptial contract limiting the husband's liability to a certain sum in case of separation invites disagreement, encourages separation, and incites divorce proceedings, thereby tending to overthrow and destroy those principles of the laws of marriage requiring that the husband and wife live

---

[1]Crouch v. Crouch, 385 S.W. 2d 288, 293

together their natural life, and that the husband, within his financial ability, shall support his wife; and because of the interest that the public has in such causes, the question of alimony is a matter for the court, and the action of the court will not be controlled by an antenuptial agreement of the parties on this subject.[2]

Shortly after the emergence of the "no-fault" divorce laws, beginning in 1969 – 70, the courts started making drastic changes in the laws governing antenuptial agreements. One of the leading cases was *Posner v. Posner,* quashed on other grounds,[3] in which the court said:

There can be no doubt that the institution of marriage is the foundation of the familial and social structure of our Nation and, as such, continues to be of vital interest to the State; but we cannot blind ourselves to the fact that the concept of the "sanctity" of a marriage — as being practically indissoluble, once entered into — held by our ancestors only a few generations ago, has been greatly eroded in the last several decades. This court can take judicial notice of the fact that the ratio of marriages to divorces has reached a disturbing rate in many states; and that a new concept of divorce — in which there is no "guilty" party — is being advocated by many groups and has been adopted by the State of California in a recent revision of its divorce laws providing for dissolution of a marriage upon pleading and proof of "irreconcilable differences" between the parties, without assessing the fault for the failure of the marriage against either party.

With such divorce such a commonplace fact of life, it is fair to assume that many prospective marriage partners whose property and familial situation is such as to generate a valid antenuptial agreement settling their property rights upon the death of either, might want to consider and discuss also — and agree upon, if possible — the disposition of their property and the alimony rights of the wife in the event their marriage, despite their best efforts, should fail.[4]

---

[2]70 A.L.R. 826, 828
[3]Posner v. Posner, 257, So. 2d. 530
[4]Ibid., 233 So. 2d. 381

The court then said:

> We have given careful consideration to the question of whether the change in public policy towards divorce requires a change in the rule respecting antenuptial agreements settling alimony and property rights of the parties upon divorce and have concluded that such agreements should no longer be held to be void ab initio as "contrary to public policy." If such an agreement is valid when tested by the stringent rules prescribed in Del Vecchio v. Del Vecchio, supra, 143 So.2d 17, for ante- and postnuptial agreements settling the property rights of the spouses in the estate of the other upon death, and if, in addition, it is made to appear that the divorce was prosecuted in good faith, on proper grounds, so that, under the rules applicable to postnuptial alimony and property settlement agreements referred to above, it could not be said to facilitate or promote the procurement of a divorce, then it should be held valid as to conditions existing at the time the agreement was made.

Courts should be extremely cautious when called upon to declare a contract void on the ground of public policy. Prejudice to the public interest must clearly appear before the court is justified in declaring a contract void as against public policy. Since it is a matter of great public concern that freedom of contract not be lightly interfered with, it is only in clear cases that contracts will be held void as contrary to public policy. Where a particular contract is not prohibited under constitutional or statutory provision, or prior judicial decision, it should not be struck down on the ground that it is contrary to public policy, unless it is clearly injurious to the public good or contravenes some established interest of society.

Consistent with the trend of the cases, many states have changed attitudes about these provisions in antenuptial agreements, and it is anticipated that most states eventually will adopt the new approach. Nevertheless, you should carefully ascertain the laws of your state before you enter upon such an agreement. It is also recommended that severability clauses be incorporated in these agreements to avoid potential invalidity of the entire agreement in the event a court should find any objectionable clauses.

You can prepare your own agreements in some cases. If, however, significant property rights are involved or there are serious problems relating to the validity of specific provisions, you should obtain competent professional advice.

Chapter 9

Common-Law Marriages

Marriage is a relationship in which the public is deeply interested, and it is subject to proper regulations and control by the state. The public policy relating to marriage is to foster and protect it, to make it a permanent and public institution, and to prevent separation and divorce. This policy has, in the past, been expressed in every state in this country in legislative enactments designed to prevent the break up of marriages for slight cause or by the agreement of the parties. Under the old divorce laws, the law usually required full and satisfactory proof of guilt or fault before permitting the dissolution of marriage.

CEREMONIAL MARRIAGE

Marriage is the civil status, condition, or relation of one man and one woman united in law for life, for the discharge to each other and the community of the duties legally incumbent on those whose association is founded on the distinction of sex. It is a *contract,* according to the form prescribed by law, by which a man and woman, capable of entering into such contract, mutually engage with each other to live their whole lives together in the state of union that ought to exist between a husband and wife.

Justification for the participation of the state in the marriage union is founded upon a paramount state interest in the continuation of the traditional family. This rationale for marriage was stated by the United States Supreme Court as follows:

> When the contracting parties have entered into the married state, they have not so much entered into a contract as into a new relation, the rights, duties, and obligations of which rest not upon their agreement, but upon the general law of the State, statutory or common, which defines and prescribes those rights, duties, and obligations.[1]

COMMON-LAW MARRIAGE

A *common-law marriage* is a nonceremonial or informal marriage by agreement, entered into by a man and a woman having capacity to marry, ordinarily without compliance with the usual statutory formalities relating to marriage licenses and ceremonial marriage. At common law, no formal ceremony of any kind was essential to a valid marriage, and an agreement between the parties, by words of the present tense or a present agreement, to be husband and wife, constituted a valid marriage. No other ceremony was necessary.

In most states where common-law marriages are valid, there are also requirements for cohabitation or a *holding themselves out to the public as husband and wife*. In other words, there must be a present agreement, and there must be actual demonstration of the marriage relationship to the general public, which normally includes cohabitation as husband and wife.

In general, the *holding themselves out as husband and wife* publicly takes the place of a ceremony. This demonstration to the general public is based on the proposition that marriage is a contract in which the public is interested, and to which the state is a party.

Some states hold that a valid common-law marriage is created as soon as the parties agree to henceforth be husband and wife, and that no time need elapse, such as for cohabitation and reputation of marital status, before the marriage is complete.

Essentially, the four basic elements of common-law marriages are: capacity of the parties to contract, present agreement to be husband and wife, a reasonable period of living as husband and wife, and reputation of marriage in the community.

---

[1]Maynard v. Hill, 125 U.S. 190 (1880)

The common-law marriage developed in this country in the early days because of the inconvenience of traveling, the immense distances between remote settlements and the few places where marriage licenses could be obtained, and the scarcity of persons authorized to perform marriage ceremonies.

Despite the judicial acceptance, in some states, of the doctrine of common-law marriages, the concept is generally frowned upon in this country in modern times. It has been declared contrary to public policy and public morals and, in view of the ease with which it can be contracted, it has been described as a fruitful source of perjury and fraud to be tolerated and not encouraged.

Nevertheless, several states recognize the validity of common-law marriages. Some states do not recognize common-law marriages, but a common-law marriage contracted in another state where they are valid is recognized in most states. These laws are subject to change, and you are cautioned to check the current status of your own state laws where appropriate.

Chapter 10

Adoption

Adoption is the legal process pursuant to state statutes in which a child's legal rights and duties toward his natural parents are terminated and similar rights and duties toward adoptive parents are substituted. It is simply the taking into your family the child of another and giving him the rights, privileges, and duties of a child and heir. The procedure is entirely statutory and has no historical basis in common law. Most adoptions are through agency placements, but court approval is generally required.

In general, adoption proceedings are uncontested and rarely generate any kind of controversy; therefore, the proceedings in court are relatively simple and devoted to protect the interests of the children and the interests of society. All of the state statutes are quite similar and are designed to afford the court sufficient information to protect the interests of all parties, including any interested persons who might have any objection to an adoption.

PETITIONS FOR ADOPTION

Typically, state statutes provide that a petition for adoption must contain certain information, which usually includes the following:

- Names, ages, and place of residence of all parties
- Dates of birth and other such information about peti-

tioners and the child, including such items as residence, citizenship, marital status, occupation, financial condition, ability to support, moral character, health, and home surroundings

- Names, residence, and other information about the child's natural parents, if any, or his guardian, if any
- Description of any property that the child owns
- Facts concerning consents or notice that might be required to be filed.
- Reasons for adoption
- Name change, if any
- Report of any adoption agency or other investigations
- Other information required by statue

Some statutes provide for the adoption of minor children only, while some statutes permit the adoption of an adult. The statutes usually provide that the adopting parents be over a certain age or a certain number of years older than the person adopted. Consent to the adoption of a minor must be given by the natural parents and by the person having legal custody, or legal cause must be shown why such consent is not required. The adopted person must consent if he is over a designated minimum age. Spouses of the adopting parties and of adopted adults must consent.

An *agreement to adopt* executed by the adopting party or parties, that the child will be adopted and treated in all respects as his own lawful child, is required by some statutes.

The applicable part of the Uniform Adoption Act, on which most state statutes are based, is as follows:

Sec 9. Petition for Adoption

(a) A petition for adoption shall be signed and verified by the petitioner, filed with the clerk of the Court, and state:

(1) the date and place of birth of the individual to be adopted, if known;

(2) The name to be used for the individual to be adopted;

(3) The date (petitioner acquired custody of the minor and) of placement of the minor and the name of the person placing the minor;

(4) the full name, age, place and duration of residence of the petitioner;

(5) the marital status of the petitioner, including the date and place of marriage, if married;

(6) that the petitioner has facilities and resources, including those available under a subsidy agreement, suitable to provide for the nurture and care of the minor to be adopted, and that it is the desire of the petitioner to establish the relationship of parent and child with the individual to be adopted;

(7) a description and estimate of value of any property of the individual to be adopted; and

(8) the name of any person whose consent to the adoption is required, but who has not consented, and facts or circumstances which excuse the lack of his consent normally required to the adoption.

(b) A certified copy of the birth certificate or verification of birth record of the individual to be adopted, if available, and the required consents and relinquishments shall be filed with the clerk.

ADOPTION OF MINORS

The method for adoption is by court proceedings pursuant to the statutes. Most statutes require the adopting party to be a resident of the state, and the proceedings must be started in the county in which the child or its parents reside, or in which the child is domiciled.

Notice

The statutes authorize the adoption of a child by strangers only in cases where:

- The natural parents consent
- The child has been abandoned by its natural parents
- It is manifestly to the interest of the child that it be taken from the parents' custody by some judicial proceeding of which the parents have notice.

According to the statutes, if the natural parents have not consented to the adoption of the child, they must be afforded an opportunity to object in an adversary proceeding in which the rights of the parents can be accorded due recognition. Generally, where consent of natural parents is not obtained, the parents are made parties to the judicial proceedings. If there are no natural parents living, the guardian of the minor children, if any, must receive notice of the proceedings.

Guardian Ad Litem

Some statutes provide for the appointment of a *guardian ad litem,* a special guardian appointed by the court to prosecute or defend, on behalf of an infant or incompetent, any suit or proceeding involving his rights. The guardian ad litem is considered an officer of the court to represent the interests of the infant or incompetent in any litigation that affects his legal rights. A guardian ad litem is used especially where the natural parents, because of mental incompetency or other reason, are incapable of giving the necessary consent to the proposed adoption of the child. In many cases, a state welfare agency or other state agency handles many of these functions.

Consent

The mother's consent to the adoption of an illegitimate child is ordinarily necessary. The father's consent is not necessary unless he acknowledges the child and marries the mother. If the parents are divorced, the adoption statutes and the custody provisions of the divorce decree determine whether one or both parents must give consent. Abandonment of a child by a parent makes consent unnecessary, as does the forfeiture of parental rights by judicial determination. The necessity of the consent of the adopted child depends on the age of the child.

After notice has been given to all interested parties, a hearing can be held and evidence submitted to support or oppose the petition, after which the court enters a judgment granting or denying the petition.

In the event a petition for adoption is contested or has controverted objections, you should obtain the services of a lawyer. Since, however, a vast majority of adoptions are uncontested and are "friendly," there is no necessity for a lawyer to handle these petitions. An adoption proceeding usually can be accomplished merely by handling the paper work as set out in the applicable statute. The following form is a general form to give you an idea of what your state statute provides. You will, of course, need to follow the particular statute in your state.

FORM 7: PETITION FOR ADOPTION OF MINOR

The petition of _____*(Name)*_____ and
_____*(Name)*_____ for adoption of the above-
named minor child respectfully shows:

    1. Petitioners are husband and wife, residing at
_____*(Address)*_____ , in the City of
_____, County of
_____, State of
_____, and each has been a resident of
the State of _____ for more than
_____*(Period of time)*_____ immediately prior to the filing of
this petition. *(State any additional information required by
statute as to date and place of marriage ceremony.)*

    2. Petitioners are of the _____ race and _____
religious faith.

    3. Petitioner, _____*(Name)*_____ , is _____ years
of age and Petitioner, _____*(Name)*_____ , is _____
years of age. *(State any additional information required by
statute as to date and place of petitioners' birth.)*

    4. The age of _____*(Name)*_____ , the
_____*(male or female)*_____ minor child sought to be adopted
by the petitioners herein, is _____ years. Said child is of the
_____ race and _____ religious faith.

    5. Said minor child resides at
_____*(Address)*_____ . *(If living with petitioners, state
how long in their custody and circumstances of placement therein.)*

    6. The names of the parents of said child are
_____*(Name)*_____ and
_____*(Name)*_____ , who reside at
_____*(Address)*_____ . *(If names of parents are
unknown, so state; if place of residence of one or both is
unknown, so state.)*

    7. The said parents consent to the adoption of said child
by petitioners, which said consent is in writing, duly executed,
and filed herewith. *(Where the consent of both parents, if living,
is not alleged, there should be allegations conforming to the
statutory provisions that would dispense with the necessity for
consent by one or both parents.)*

    8. *(Statement as to legal custody of child, if in one parent, in
guardian, child-placement agency, etc., and allegation of consent
of such custodian to adoption.)*

9. Petitioner, _____(Name)_____, is the
_____(Relationship)_____ of said minor child. *(If petitioner or petitioners have no relationship to the child, so state.)*

10. A full description of the property of said child is as follows: _____.

11. Petitioners desire that the relationship of parent and child be established between them and the child, it being to the best interest of the child to be adopted by them. *(Follow with any required statement as to the good moral character and financial status of the petitioners.)*

12. *(Allegation of report by appropriate person or agency, favorable to adoption or temporary custody of child pending adoption.)*

14. *(Allegation of child's consent to the adoption, when of the age that such consent is required by statute.)*

15. All necessary consents *(If appropriate, add: and the agreement for adoption are annexed hereto and made a part hereof.)*

16. *(Any other allegations required under the statutes of customary in the practice of the particular jurisdiction.)*

Wherefore, petitioners pray this court for an order granting leave to adopt as their own child the said _____(Name)_____, and that from and after the date of such order the said child be decreed and considered, for all legal purposes, the child of said petitioners; that the said child be rendered capable of inheriting the estate of petitioners; that the name of the said child be changed to _____(Name)_____, pursuant to the statute in such case made and provided; and that all orders may be made in the premises as this court may seem fit and proper according to law. (Signature, Verification, etc.)

Chapter 11

Change of Name

Your name is very important to you and your family. It is very personal, it is a phenomenon, an event, a "happening," a constant companion that goes with you from the beginning to the end. It is capable of generating pride and prejudice, of winning a smile or a smirk. It reflects your personality and character. We like to think it carries a touch of magic, of romance, and of enchantment. Most of us have had no choice in the selection of our names. Many people would like to adopt another name if they can do it legally, but they think it is a big legal hassle.

It is easier than you think to legally change your name.

Your name is a title by which you are called or designated, in distinction from other persons in society, and it serves as a label that you bear for the convenience of the world at large in addressing you. It is a general custom for a person to have one first name (Christian name or given name) and one last name (surname or family name). Most people have one middle name or initial, and some people have one or more additional names. Those who have served in the military service, prisons, or other such organizations also have numbers by which they are known.

COMMON-LAW RIGHT

In the absence of a statute to the contrary, a person may change his name at any time without any legal proceedings merely by adopting another name. This easy method of changing your name should not, however, be abused or misunderstood. The law does not permit a name change for fraudulent or unlawful purposes. Even though it is quite easy to change your name by this common-law rule, it is recommended that you use your state's statutory legal proceedings to document your change of name and ensure full "legal" status to the change. Each time you change your name, it is generally necessary to notify various governmental agencies (Social Security office; Internal Revenue Service; voting registrar; automobile registrars; real estate, stock, bond, etc. offices) and other persons or entities with whom you deal or communicate. It is easier to change your name than it is to "notify the world" of your new name.

STATUTORY METHOD FOR CHANGE OF NAME

Under the common law, a person can change his surname without any formal legal proceedings, so long as the purpose is not fraudulent and the change does not infringe upon another's rights. All states, however, provide a statutory method for effecting a change of name, which usually requires that some type of notice be given to interested parties. Most states hold that the statutory procedure is merely supplemental to, and not supplanting, the common-law method. Some states, however, (about eight) hold that the statutory method is the exclusive way for a person to change his name. It is quite easy to review your state's statute to determine the procedures and requirements.

The applicable statutes generally provide for the filing of a written petition or application giving certain information about the petitioner and the reasons for the change of name. The petition also states that there is no fraudulent or unlawful intent or reason for the change.

The statutes do not repeal or change the common-law right to change a name; they merely afford a formal procedural method for effecting a change. It is speedy and definite, and it affords a formal record by which the change of name is established with a formal declaration of the court.

The statutes usually are worded so as to give the courts reasonable discretion in granting or denying the petition for change of name. The court may not abuse its discretion, and if it does it is subject to reversal on appeal. Some cases discussed later in this chapter demonstrate this rule.

The general rule is that some substantial reason must exist before the court is justified in denying a petition for change of name. The court is not subject to every whim of every petitioner for change of name, but generally will grant the petition in absence of some reasonable objection to the change. Thus, it has been held that a petition for change of name was properly denied on the ground that it also would change the name of petitioner's wife and children. Also, the refusal of a married woman's petition for change of name to that of her deceased former husband for the sole purpose of prosecuting a wrongful death action was proper. The fact that an applicant for a change of name has been discharged in bankruptcy and has not paid the debts in the bankruptcy proceedings has been held not sufficient to deny an application for change of name.

The statutes provide for the filing of a written petition in a court of record. The petition usually gives the name, date and place of birth, age, and residence of the petitioner; the name that he wants to adopt; and the reason for the change. The petition should be verified, that is, signed under oath. Some statutes require information as to whether the petitioner has been convicted of a crime, has been adjudged bankrupt, has judgments or liens of record, has any lawsuits pending against him. If any of those situations are true, other facts and details might be required. The courts may deny a petition that does not comply fully with the formal requirements of the statutes; thus, you should pay particular attention to the specific requirements of your own state's statutes.

Some petitions might be granted without a hearing; however, most require a short evidentiary hearing to support the granting of a change. If no objections are made, it is usually routine. If objections are made by any party, the judge will decide the issue based on the evidence presented. The evidence must be sufficient for the court to make a determination regarding the issues presented in the petition.

CHANGE OF NAME OF MINORS

Statutes providing for change of name proceedings sometimes stipulate that where the change of a minor's name is sought, both parents, if surviving, must join in the petition. In these instances, it has been held that the consent of both parents is a necessary prerequisite to the change of name. Such statutes, however, have been held not to apply in some circumstances, such as when the parent opposing the change has been guilty of gross misconduct, or the child was born out of wedlock or during the pendency of a separation action. On the other hand, statutes sometimes provide that a single parent, upon giving proper notice to the other, may petition for a change of name of their minor child. Under such a statute, it has been held that the consent of both parents is not essential.

In determining whether a change in a child's name should be permitted or ordered against the objection or without the consent of one of the parents, the courts usually have recognized that the welfare of the child should be the controlling consideration, and that the determination of the issues involved is ordinarily a matter within the discretion of the court.

A father, who is ordinarily the objecting party, has a protectible interest in having his child bear the paternal surname in accordance with the usual custom. This interest obtains even if the mother has been awarded custody of the child by a judicial decree. Some courts also have held, however, that the interest of the father in having his child bear the paternal surname is not sufficient to deny the name change. Because the father's interest in having the child bear the paternal surname is usually given significant consideration in weighing his opposition to the change, the contention that a child's name should be changed merely to save the mother from inconvenience, embarrassment, or confusion is ordinarily given little or no consideration. It has been recognized, however, that there is merit in the contention that a mother has a right, equal to that of the father, in having the child bear her maiden name.

In applying these considerations in particular proceedings involving the change of a child's name that is opposed by one of the parents, the courts have reached different results. The difference in the court cases is based on the evidence presented; therefore, it is advisable for you to prepare your evidence well if there is likely to be any objection to your petition.

TYPICAL STATE STATUTES

The Colorado Statutes on Name Changes are typical of other states' statutes, and are quoted here for your review.

13-15-101. Petition — proceedings. Every person desiring to change his name may present a petition to that effect, verified by affidavit, to the district, superior, or county court in the county of the petitioner's residence. The petition shall set forth the petitioner's full name, the new name desired, and a concise statement of the reason for such desired change. The court shall order such change to be made, and spread upon the records of the court in proper form, if the court is satisfied that the desired change would be proper, and not detrimental to the interests of another person.

13-15-102. Publication of change. Public notice of such change of name shall be given at least three times in a newspaper published in the county where such person is residing within twenty days after the order of the court is made, and if no newspaper is published in that county, such notice shall be published in a newspaper in such county as the court directs.

TYPICAL COURT CASES

You might wish to review some of the court cases in your state applying the statutes to specific cases. You can simply check the annotations (cases) cited in the statutes of your own state. You can find these in any law library or lawyer's office. The following review of leading cases will give you a good idea of how the courts apply the statutes.

Case 1. In a Missouri case, a 27-year-old man filed a change of name petition seeking to change his name from Morris Edward Reed to Sunshine Morris Edward Reed. He asserted that he is known by his friends and associates as Sunshine, that he uses the name Sunshine in the conduct of his daily affairs, that he prefers the name Sunshine over his given name, and that he had used that name in his employment for several years. The trial court denied the petition, but the appeal court reversed and held that the desired change would be proper and not detrimental to the interests of any other person.[1]

Case 2. Indiana: Petitioner was married to Denis J. Hauptly and had adopted the use of his name. She filed a petition seeking to change her name from her married name to her

---

[1]584 S.W. 2d. 103

maiden name, Elizabeth Marie Howard. Her husband agreed to the change. At the hearing she testified that she was unhappy with the name of Hauptly in that she felt it hid her true identity and heritage. She appeared to be quite proud of her maiden name and the ethnic background that it represented. She testified that she was not seeking the name change in order to perpetrate fraud on anyone, to hide her identity from any creditors, or to escape identification for any criminal action. The trial court denied her petition, and the appeal court reversed, holding:

> There is no statutory requirement in Indiana that the petitioner establish any particular reason other than his personal desire for change of name. There is, of course, the common law restriction that a name change should not be permitted in order to defraud others or to hide criminal activity.
> . . . In fact, there is no legal requirement that any person go through the courts to establish a legal change of name. The statute merely provides for an orderly record of the change of name in order to avoid future confusion. In the absence of a statute, a person may ordinarily change his name at will without any legal proceedings. The person need only adopt another name. This may be done so long as the change of name is not done for a fraudulent purpose.[2]

Case 3. In a Texas case, Marguerite Lynn Erickson filed a petition to change her married name, Erickson, back to her maiden name, McGregor. There were no objections to the petition; however, the trial court denied the petition. The appeal court reversed and granted the petition, saying:

> In light of the general policy of most courts in other states to grant requests for change of name, we feel that the appellant presented sufficient 'good cause' for granting her application as required by section 32.22. It is enough that, for her own proper reasons, appellant conscientiously feels the necessity of being known and referred to by her previous name. To deny her this right would be a violation of equal protec-

---

[2]312 N.E. 2d 857

tion under the law by creating an invalid classification based on sex.[3]

Case 4. Walter Knight, an inmate of the State Prison, petitioned the district court to change his name to Sundiata Simba. His reasons were "to acknowledge the heritage of his past, and to fortify his acceptance of his religious beliefs as required by his faith." The trial court denied the petition, and the appeal court reversed. The appeal court said:

> At common law, a person could adopt another name at will. Statutes setting forth procedures to be followed in changing a name merely provide an additional method for making the change . . . While a court has wide discretion in matters of this type, it should not deny the application for change of name as being improper unless special circumstances or facts are found to exist. Included in these would be 'unworthy motive, the possibility of fraud on the public, or the choice of a name that is bizarre, unduly lengthy, ridiculous or offensive to common decency and good taste'. . . Likewise, there is authority to deny the change if the interests of a wife or child of the applicant would be adversely affected thereby . . .[4]

Case 5. Michael Herbert Dengler filed a petition to change his name to "1069." The trial court denied the petition and the appeal court affirmed. The appeal court said:

> In this court he assigns no reasons for the selection of "1069" beyond stating that it has personal significance and relates to his unique philosophy. He argued below that the number "1069" symbolized his interrelationship with society, and conceptually reflected his personal and philosophical identity . . . We affirm for the reason that we are satisfied it was not the intention of the legislatuee . . . to authorize a court order which changes to a numeral and alphabetical 'name' as that word has been historically and traditionally understood.

The court stated, however:

---

[3]547 S.W. 2d. 357
[4]537 P. 2d. 1085, Colorado

Meanwhile, as we have indicated, the appellant is at liberty to enjoy his common law right to the use of numerals as his name, as long as he is willing to endure the inconvenience which is attendant on asserting the right.[5]

[5]287 N.W. 2d. 637, Minnesota

FORM 8: PETITION FOR CHANGE OF NAME

IN THE _____ COURT

COUNTY OF _____

No. _____

STATE OF _____

Petition for Change of Name

In the matter of Petition of

_____*(Existing Name)*_____

to Change name to

_____*(Desired Name)*_____

Petitioner alleges:

1. Petitioner's name is _____*(Existing Name)*_____ and resides at _____*(Address)*_____ City of _____, County of _____, State of _____.

2. Petitioner's birth date, place of birth, and residence during the past _____ years are as follows: _____
_____
_____

A certified copy of petitioner's birth certificate is attached hereto and made a part hereof.

3. Petitioner's marital status and the names and addresses of petitioner's parents, spouse, if any, children, if any, and next of kin are as follows: _____
_____
_____

4. Petitioner desires to change his/her name to _____*(Desired Name)*_____ for the following reasons:
_____
_____
_____
_____
_____

5. There are no reasonable objections to said change of name, and it would not be detrimental to the interests of any person, to society, or to the state.

6. All procedural requirements of the applicable statute have been complied with, including the following: _____
_____
_____

7. Additional information required by the applicable statute is as follows: _____
_____
_____

Wherefore, petitioner requests the entry of an order changing his/her name from _____*(Existing Name)*_____ to _____*(Desired Name)*_____ .

_____*(Signature)*_____
Petitioner

COUNTY OF _____
STATE OF _____

Sworn to and subscribed before me this _____ day of _____, 19_____.

_____*(Signature)*_____
Notary Public

Chapter 12

How to Win
Landlord-Tenant Disputes

One of the dominant factors in our business, professional, social, and political activities is real estate. The development, use, financing, repair, maintenance, sale, lease, and management of real estate has accounted for a large part of the country's economy. The renting of an apartment, a home, or other residential dwelling is one of the most personal things in "real estate" dealings for most of us. It is also one of the most expensive items in our budget. The relationship of the landlord and the tenant is as delicate and sensitive as that of the husband and wife; they both involve a marriage that very easily can burst into flames. The law, in its function of regulating the activities among the people in our society, recently has gone through some rather remarkable changes.

In fact, over 200 years of well established law have been reversed during the past 5 to 10 years. Both the judicial and legislative branches of both federal and state government have made dramatic, sudden, and significant changes. These new and different rules are said to be more equitable and more compatible with the reality of our modern society.

The relationship of landlord and tenant is created by contract. It can be a contract either express or implied, written or verbal, and typically provides that one person, designated the *tenant*, enters into possession of the premises of another person, known as the *landlord*. The tenant occupies the premises of the landlord, in subordination of the landlord's title and right of reversion. The contract or agreement is generally in writing and is called a *lease.*

The essential elements of a lease, the creation of a landlord and tenant relationship, are:

- Competent parties
- Description of the real estate demised
- Terms
- Rent

Although these are the bare legal essentials of a lease, it is rare that a lease is limited to these four items. Other items that might be included in a typical lease are discussed later in this chapter. These lease provisions can be rather lengthy. The key to your success in negotiating and drafting a good lease depends upon your being able to cover those items that are likely to be pertinent to your situation. As a prospective tenant, you can avoid many unnecessary and vexing disputes, quarrels, and potential lawsuits if you study carefully and discuss in detail with the landlord each of the items involved in your lease. Even in those rare situations in which disputes cannot be avoided, or in which you do not prevail, you will be in a much better position to win your case if you know about the typical pitfalls and are able to negotiate in good faith with the landlord. Once you become familiar with the applicable laws, you will be in a favorable position to write a good lease, or to make appropriate changes in the standard form leases.

TYPES OF TENANCIES

There are four kinds of interests in land that are generally referred to as tenancies. They are: tenancy for a term, periodic tenancy, tenancy at will, and tenancy at sufferance.

Tenancy for a Term

A *tenancy for a term,* or a tenancy for years or estate for years, as it is sometimes called, arises when the two parties agree that the tenant will hold the property for a certain length of time, and no longer. Every estate that must expire at a period certain and fixed in advance, by whatever words created, is an estate for years. It is a cardinal principle in the creation of terms for years that the term must be certain; that is, there must be certainty as to the commencement and the duration of the term. A lease is the classic example; it gives the tenant the right to possess the property for 6 months or 1 year or 5 years or 99 years.

Periodic Tenancies

The tenancy from period to period, or *periodic tenancy,* arises when the parties agree that a specific rent will be paid by the tenant — for example, every week, every month, or every year — but do not make any agreement as to when the tenancy will end. That is, the tenancy will normally continue from period to period indefinitely so long as the rent is paid, and so long as the lease is not otherwise terminated.

In most states, the period of a tenancy is measured according to the interval over which the rent is paid. Thus, a weekly rent creates a tenancy from week to week; a monthly rent makes a tenancy from month to month. Occasionally the period is based upon how the rent is calculated (or estimated), rather how it is paid. Thus, a rent of $1,200 per year, payable $100 per month, could be regarded as creating either a tenancy from year to year, or a tenancy from month to month. You can easily remove any ambiguity by specifying your desires and intentions in the lease.

Tenancy at Will

A *tenancy at will* arises when a landowner permits another person to possess the property without any agreement between them as to a termination date or as to payment of rent. An estate at will in lands is that which a tenant has, by an entry made thereon under a demise, to hold during the joint wills of the parties. The chief characteristics of a tenancy at will are uncertainty respecting the term and the right of either party to terminate it by proper notice, and these features must exist whether the tenancy is created by the express language of the contract or by implication of law.

Tenancy at Sufferance

A person becomes a *tenant at sufferance* by holding over after the expiration of the term without the prior consent of the landlord. If the landlord permits the tenancy and accepts rent from the tenant, the tenant becomes a periodic tenant. If the landlord orders the tenant to leave and sues to recover possession, and the tenant remains in possession, he becomes a trespasser.

TERMINATION OF TENANCIES

Regulations on the termination of a tenancy differ among the types of tenancies.

Tenancy for a Term

One of the attributes of a lease for a term is the specification of a definite period after which the lease is automatically at an end. Therefore, no notice is required for terminating these leases.

Periodic Tenancies

The periodic tenancy will automatically renew unless a timely notice of termination is given by one of the parties. Usually the notice must be given at least one period in advance. A tenancy from week to week usually requires 7 days notice of termination; a tenancy from month to month usually requires 30 days notice.

Some state statutes permit the parties to agree to a shorter notice period, and some statutes prohibit short notices in some circumstances. The current trend in most states is to adopt more restrictive laws that protect tenants from unfair treatment by managers and owners of multidwellings.

Tenancies at Will

At common law, no advance notice was necessary to terminate a tenancy at will. Most state statutes now require some advance notice, thereby making this estate very similar to the periodic tenancy.

Tenancies at Sufferance

No notice should be required by the landlord to end this tenancy since the tenant is already past the original termination date. If however, the holdover becomes a periodic tenant by virtue of the landlord's election, then the estate must be terminated in the same way as all other periodic tenancies.

IMPLIED WARRANTY OF HABITABILITY

The legal principles of this country, until a few years ago, regarded the relationship of landlord and tenant as one governed by the precepts and doctrines of property law. In our modern society, however, the agrarian concept of landlord-tenant law has lost its credence and has become increasingly less representative of the relationship existing between the lessor and lessee. The modern tenant is more concerned with habitability than the possibility of the landlord's interference with his possession. The present-day dweller, in seeking the combination of living space, suitable facilities, and tenant services, has changed the basic function of the lease. The importance of the lease of an apartment today is not to create a tenurial relationship between the parties, but rather to arrange the leasing of a habitable dwelling.

Three things have occurred during the past few years to motivate the courts and the legislative bodies to adopt the implied warranty of habitability:

- Legislatures have now recognized that public policy requires landlords to make dwellings offered for rent safe and fit for human habitation.
- The landlord has a superior knowledge of the condition of the premises he leases to the tenant. Housing code requirements, and their violations, are usually known, or notice of them is given to the landlord. The landlord is in a better position than the tenant to know of latent defects in the wiring, plumbing, or structure. Those defects might go unnoticed by the tenant, who rarely has sufficient knowledge or experience to discover them.
- It is appropriate that the landlord should bear the cost of repairs to make the premises safe and suitable for human habitation. If he does not, the result could be the rental of poor housing facilities in violation of public policy.

The rule of law applicable in all states prior to the adoption of the implied warranty of habitability doctrine was stated in *Ingalls v. Hobbs*[1] as follows:

It is well settled, both in this commonwealth and in England,

---

[1] Ingalls v. Hobbs, 156 Mass. 348, 349, 350, 31 N.E. 286, (1892)

116

that one who lets an unfurnished building to be occupied as a dwelling house does not impliedly agree that it is fit for habitation. (citing cases) In the absence of fraud or a covenant, the purchaser of real estate, or the hirer of it for a term, however short, takes it as it is, and determines for himself whether it will serve the purpose for which he wants it.

Some states have enacted statutes on the implied warranty of habitability, and some have changed the laws by court decisions; some have done both. The statement of the modern implied warranty of habitability rule is reflected in the syllabus of the court in the case of *Teller v. McCoy*[2] as follows:

1. There is, in a written or oral lease of residential premises, an implied warranty that the landlord shall at the commencement of a tenancy deliver the dwelling unit and surrounding premises in a fit and habitable condition and shall thereafter maintain the leased property in such condition.

2. Since a lease of a residential dwelling is to be treated as a contract, the covenant to pay rent is dependent upon the premises being habitable. The tenant's duty to pay rent is dependent upon the landlord's fulfillment of the implied warranty of habitability.

3. Breach of the implied warranty of habitability may constitute a defense to an action for unlawful detainer or to an action for rent or damages brought by the landlord.

4. If a landlord breaches the implied warranty of habitability, the tenant may vacate the premises thereby terminating his obligation to pay rent or may continue to pay rent and bring his own action or counterclaim later to recover damages caused by the breach.

5. When the warranty of habitability is breached, the tenant's damages are measured by the differences between the fair market value of the premises if they had been so warranted and the fair rental value of the premises as they were during the occupancy by the tenant in the unsafe and

---

[2]Teller v. McCoy, 253 S.E. 2d. 114 (West Virginia)

unsanitary condition. However, the tenant may additionally recover damages for annoyance and inconvenience proven to have resulted from the breach.

6. The trial court, after determining that a fact question exists as to a breach of warranty of habitability, may, during the pendency of the action, require the tenant in possession to make future rent payments or part thereof into an escrow account as they become due, but only in limited circumstances, only on motion of the landlord, and only after notice and opportunity for a hearing on such a motion.

7. Waiver of the implied warranty of habitability is prohibited as against public policy.

Some courts have established additional rights for the tenant, including the following:

1. Upon the landlord's failure of performance, the tenant can perform it at his own expense and deduct the cost of such performance from the amount of rent due and payable; or

2. The tenant can surrender the possession of the premises to relieve himself from any further payment of rent; or

3. He can retain possession of the premises and deduct from the rent the difference between the rental value of the premises as it would have been if the lease had been fully complied with by the landlord and its rental value in the condition it actually was.

Where the implied warranty of habitability is adopted by the courts, rather than by statutes, another problem is presented: how to enforce the new rights given to the tenant.
One court made the following observation:

To constitute a breach of the implied warranty of habitability, the lessee should be required to bring the defects to the attention of the lessor and give him a reasonable time to remedy them. The defects should be of such a nature as rendered the living quarters unsafe, unsanitary, or uninhabitable. Where there has been a material breach of implied warranty of habitability with respect to residential property, tenant's damages should be measured by the difference between the fair rental value of the premises, if they had been as warranted and the fair rental value of the premises as they were during occupancy by the tenant in the unsafe or unsanitary condition. When a tenant vacates the premise because of the landlord's breach, the condition of the premises should lose its relevance after the vacation for the damages should be determined on the basis of the fair value during the tenant's occupancy.

Not every defect or inconvenience should be deemed to constitute a breach of covenant of habitability; the condition complained of should be such as truly renders the premises uninhabitable in the eyes of a reasonable person. The following factors have been considered material by other courts in determining whether there has been a material breach of the implied warranty of habitability:
1. the nature of the deficiency or defect;
2. its effect on safety and sanitation;
3. the length of time for which it persisted;
4. the age of the structure;
5. the amount of rent;
6. whether tenant voluntarily, knowingly, and intelligently waived the defects, or is estopped to raise the question of the breach;
7. whether the defects or deficiencies resulted from unusual, abnormal, or malicious use by the tenant; and
8. whether the alleged defect would be such as to violate housing laws, regulations or ordinances.[3]

EXCULPATORY CLAUSES IN RESIDENTIAL LEASES

An *exculpatory clause* is a provision in a lease in which the landlord is released from liability for his own negligent acts or wrongful conduct. Until recently, a vast majority of the courts have held these clauses to be valid and enforceable, even though they expressly exempt the landlord from liability in connection with the leased premises resulting from the landlord's negligence, the negligence of the landlord's agents and

---

[3]Steele v. Latimer, 214 Kan 329, 521 P. 2d. 304, 311 (Kansas)

servants, damages generally, or damages from certain specified causes.

The reasoning behind the rule is based upon the doctrine of freedom of contract, which rests squarely upon significant provisions of the federal and state constitutions. It has been suggested that the freedom of contract doctrine as applied to real-estate lease exculpatory clauses is an apparent conflict with, and is subservient to, the basic principle that a landlord should be liable for the negligent breach of a duty that is owed to his tenant. Those who advocate the validity of the old rule reason that the relationship of landlord and tenant is in no event a matter of public interest, but is purely a private affair, so that such clauses cannot be held void on purely public-policy grounds. The rule of validity of exculpatory clauses has not been adopted and applied in all states. In fact, the modern trend is toward holding such clauses to be against public policy.

One of the most recent decisions in the trend toward invalidating exculpatory clauses in residential leases is the decision of the California Supreme Court in Henrioulle v. Marin Ventures, Inc.,[4] entered shortly after the legislature had enacted the rule by statute. The tenant, Henrioulle, brought an action against the landlord for personal injuries. The printed form lease agreement that the tenant signed contained the following exculpatory clause:

INDEMNIFICATION: Owner shall not be liable for any damage or injury to Tenant, or any other person, or to any property, occurring on the premises, or any part thereof, or in the common areas thereof, and Tenant agrees to hold Owner harmless from any claims for damages no matter how caused.

The jury awarded damages to the tenant; however, the trial court set aside the judgment on the basis of the exculpatory clause in the lease and entered a judgment for the landlord.

On appeal, the California Supreme Court said:

Since the residential lease transaction entered into by the parties exhibits all of the characteristics of a relationship that "affects the public interest" under Tunkl, the exculpa-

---

[4]Henrioulle v. Marin Ventures, Inc., 143 Cal. Rptr. 247, 573 P. 2d. 465

tory clause cannot operate to relieve the landlord of liability in this case.

In holding that exculpatory clauses in residential leases violate public policy, this court joins an increasing number of jurisdictions (See, e.g., Kuzmiak v. Brookchester, Inc. (1955), 33 N.J. Super, 575, 111 A.2d 425; Old Town Development Co. v. Langford (Ind. App. 1976) 349 N.E. 2d 744; Weaver v. American Oil Co. (Ind. 1971) 176 N.E. 2d 144 [such clauses are void in all leases]; Papakalos v. Shaka (1941) 91 N.H. 254, 18 A.2d 377, 379 [such clauses are void in all contracts]; Billie Knitwear, Inc. v. New York Life Ins. Co. (N.Y. Sup. 1940) 174 Misc. 978, 22 N.Y.S.2d 324, affd. (1942) 288 N.Y. 682, 42 N.E. 2d 80 [such clauses invalidated by statute in all leases]; see generally, Annot., Validity of Exculpatory Clause in Lease Exempting Lessor from Liability (1971) 49 A.L.R. 3d 321.) Indeed, in 1975 the California Legislature enacted Civil Code section 1953, which declared invalid exculpatory clauses in residential leases executed on or after January 1, 1976.[5]

A number of states have enacted statutes that abrogate entirely, or to some degree, the common law concept of freedom of contracts as applied to exculpatory clauses exempting landlords from liability for their own negligence. The courts, in applying these statutes, have uniformly refused to give effect to an immunity provision exempting the landlord from liability for his own negligence. In other words, where the statute is adopted, it automatically voids all exculpatory clauses in that state. In a few of these cases, the courts have observed that, although an individual contract exempting the landlord from liability for his own negligence might not be of any public concern, the existence of a large number of similar agreements, particularly in urban residential dwellings, would clearly be of great public concern. The courts also observed that the statutes constitute an expression of the public policy of the state.

In the final analysis, it does appear that most states have adopted, are in the process of adopting, or soon will adopt, the new rule of law with respect to residential dwellings. Whether the law should be adopted by court decision or by the legislature will continue to be debated, but by whatever means is utilized, it appears to be the emerging new law.

---

[5]Civ. Code, Section 9153, Stats. 1975, ch. 302, Section 1; p. 749

RETALIATORY EVICTIONS

Retaliatory eviction occurs when a tenant is evicted because of his lawful attempt to compel his landlord to comply with the housing laws. In recent years, housing codes and regulations have been enacted setting forth various safety and sanitary standards with which a landlord must comply. The purpose and objectives of these regulations are to upgrade the quality of housing, which depends largely upon private initiative in reporting code violations to authorities.

Judicial and legislative response to a landlord's indiscriminate use of the power to evict a tenant without explanation has been the creation of the doctrine of retaliatory eviction. Following the lead of the courts, a majority of the states have enacted legislation, based largely on the Uniform Residential Landlord and Tenant Act, making the defense of retaliatory eviction available to the tenant under certain specific circumstances.

The applicable provision of the Uniform Act is as follows:

Section 5.101 Retaliatory Conduct Prohibited

(a) Except as provided in this section, a landlord may not retaliate by increasing rent or decreasing services or by bringing or threatening to bring an action for possession after:
(1) the tenant has complained to a governmental agency charged with responsibility for enforcement of a building or housing code of a violation applicable to the premises materially affecting health and safety; or
(2) the tenant has complained to the landlord of a violation under Section 2.104; or
(3) the tenant has organized or become a member of a tenant's union or similar organization.

(b) if the landlord acts in violation of subsection (a), the tenant is entitled to the remedies provided in Section 4.107 and has a defense in any retaliatory action against him for possession. In an action by or against the tenant, evidence of a complaint within [1] year before the alleged act of retaliation creates a presumption that the landlord's conduct was in retaliation. The presumption does not arise if the tenant made the complaint after notice of a proposed rent increase or diminution of services. "Presumption" means that the trier of fact must find the existence of the fact presumed unless and until evidence is introduced which would support a finding of its nonexistence.

(c) Notwithstanding subsections (a) and (b), a landlord may bring an action for possession if:

(1) the violation of the applicable building or housing code was caused primarily by the lack of reasonable care by the tenant, a member of his family, or other person on the premises with his consent; or

(2) the tenant is in default in rent; or

(3) compliance with the applicable building or housing, code requires alteration, remodeling, or demolition which would effectively deprive the tenant of the use of the dwelling unit.

(d) The maintenance of an action under subsection (c) does not release the landlord from liability under Section 4.101(b).

LEASES

It is most important for you to know and understand your legal rights and the local, state, and federal legislation pertaining to leases. It is also essential for you to know how to protect those rights and, if appropriate, remedy any wrong that may occur. It is equally important for you to understand the laws governing contracts because most landlord-tenant relationships arise through the execution of a lease. Most leases are preprinted forms used by the landlord. Many of the "form" leases are bad for the tenant and good for the landlord.

As noted, many courts hold that it is against public policy for a tenant to waive the implied warranty of habitability granted by statutes. The exculpatory clause is also highly questionable, and many courts hold that unfair or unconscionable provisions are invalid. Typically, form leases provide for the tenant to indemnify the landlord for all kinds of liabilities and responsibilities. You should watch out for these provisions in leases, and be in a position to protect your legal rights.

Chapter 13

How to Get a No-Fault Divorce Without A Lawyer

This chapter gives you a look at the history of marriage and divorce laws in America, explains the laws regulating divorce, and tells you how to handle the easy step-by-step procedures to get a no-fault divorce without a lawyer. With the ever increasing divorce rate, the money that Americans can save in attorney's fees by getting their own divorces could balance the national budget.

You will be surprised to learn how easy it is for people to get a no-fault divorce without a lawyer. The no-fault laws, enacted in virtually all states, are familiar to most people. Several states have already adopted a more simplified system for no-fault divorces by permitting the entire process to be handled by affidavit. This process avoids the need for a court appearance, and obviously eliminates the need for a lawyer — unless you have serious problems filling in blank forms. Of course, if you have any controversy or major financial transactions in connection with a divorce, you might need a lawyer.

Most of the no-fault divorce statutes provide for the dissolution of a marriage upon the showing that the marriage is irretrievably broken, or some similar description. Some of the other terms used in the various statutes include:

- Irreconcilable differences
- Upon a finding that the marriage relationship is no longer viable

- Irremedial breakdown
- Unsupportable because of discord or conflict of personalities that destroys the legitimate ends of the marriage relationship and prevents a reasonable expectation of reconciliation
- Incompatibility or incompatibility of temperament.

A *irretrievably broken marriage* is one in which either or both parties are unable or refuse to cohabit and there are no prospects of reconciliation. The question in such proceedings is whether or not the marriage is in fact ended because of the basic unsuitability of the spouses for each other and their state of mind toward the relationship.

To be irremedial, a difference does not necessarily have to be so viewed by both parties. If one marital partner has made the considered decision that the relationship should be terminated, it may properly be said that the marital relationship is broken down.

The question under the statutes relating to an irretrievably broken marriage is simply whether or not, for whatever reason or cause, no matter whose fault, or irrespective of any fault, the marriage relationship is for all intents and purposes ended, is no longer viable, or is a hollow sham beyond hope of reconciliation or repair.

Incompatibility, or incompatibility of temperament, has been defined as a conflict in the personalities or temperaments of the parties that is so deep and irreconcilable as to make it impossible for them to continue a normal marital relationship. Incompatibility, to constitute a ground for divorce, must be so great that the parties find it impossible to continue a normal marital relationship with each other. The conflict of personalities and disposition must be so deep as to be irreconcilable and irremediable.

The word *irretrievable* is defined in the dictionary as *impossible to recoup, repair, or overcome.*

The underlying purposes of the new no-fault statutes are:

- To strengthen and preserve the integrity of marriage and safeguard family relationships
- To promote the amicable settlement of disputes that have arisen between parties to a marriage
- To mitigate the potential harm to the spouses and their

children caused by the process of legal dissolution of marriage
- To make reasonable provision for the spouse and minor children during and after litigation
- To make the laws of legal dissolution of marriage effective for dealing with the relations of matrimonial experience by making irretrievable breakdown of the marriage relationship the sole basis for its dissolution
- To remove from domestic relations litigation the issue of marital fault as a determining factor
- To abolish the necessity of presenting sordid and ugly details of conduct on the part of either of the parties in order to obtain a dissolution of marriage
- To replace the concept of fault with marriage failure or irreconcilable breakdown as a basis for a decree dissolving a marriage.

Although varying in their terminology, these statutes basically provide for a dissolution of the marital relationship without regard to the fault of the parties, where it is determined that the underlying relationship of the spouses to each other has broken down to the extent that a marriage exists in name only, and that there appears to be no hope of reconciliation. Thus, such statutes shift the focus of inquiry of the court from the acts and characteristics of the parties to the state of the marriage relationship itself.

The no-fault laws adopt some new terminology. In the new laws, the term *dissolution of marriage* is used instead of the term *divorce; alimony* is now called *maintenance*. Other changes have been made, but we will use the terms interchangeably because some states continue to use the old terminology.

MARRIAGE AND DIVORCE IN AMERICA

Marriage is a relationship in which the public is deeply interested and which is subject to proper regulations and control by the state. The public policy relating to marriage is to foster and protect it, to make it a permanent and public institution, and to prevent separation and divorce. This policy has, in the past, been expressed in every state in this country in legislative enactments designed to prevent the break up of marriages for slight cause, or by the agreement of the parties. Under the old divorce statutes, the law usually required full and satisfactory proof of guilt or fault before permitting the dissolution of marriage.

Marriage is the civil status, condition, or relation of one man and one woman united in law for life, for the discharge to each other and to the community of the duties legally required of those whose association is founded on the distinction of sex. It is a contract, according to the form prescribed by law, by which a man and woman, capable of entering into such a contract, mutually engage with each other to live their whole lives together in the state of union that ought to exist between a husband and wife.

Justification for the participation of the state in the marriage union is founded upon a paramount state interest in the continuation of the traditional family. The rationale for the marriage laws is stated in an opinion of the U.S. Supreme Court in *Maynard v. Hill:*[1]

> When the contract to marry is executed by marriage, a relation between the parties is created which they cannot change. Other contracts may be modified, restricted or enlarged, or entirely released upon the consent of the parties. Not so with marriage. The relation once formed, the law steps in and holds the parties to various obligations and liabilities. It is an institution, in the maintenance of which in its purity the public is deeply interested, for it is the foundation of the family and society, without which there would be neither civilization nor progress.

> When the contracting parties have entered into the married state, they have not so much entered into a contract as into a new relation, the rights, duties, and obligations of which rest not upon their agreement, but upon the general law of the State, statutory or common, which defines and prescribes those rights, duties, and obligations. They are of law, not of contract. It was of contract that the relation should be established, but, being established, the power of the parties as to its extent or duration is at an end. Their rights under it are determined by the will of the sovereign, as evidenced by law ***. It is not, then, a contract within the meaning of the

---

[1]Maynard v. Hill, 125 U.S. 190 (1888)

clause of the Constitution which prohibits the impairing of the obligation of contracts. It is, rather, a social relation like that of parent and child, the obligations of which arise not from the consent of concurring minds, but are the creation of the law itself; a relation the most important, as affecting the happiness of individuals, the first step from barbarism to incipient civilization, the purest tie of social life and the true basis of human progress.

NO-FAULT DIVORCE LAWS AND THE UNIFORM MARRIAGE AND DIVORCE ACT

Marriage can be, and frequently is, one of the most exciting, deeply emotional, and happy events in a person's lifetime. It can be a lofty, soft, and gentle entry into the most joyous, blissful state of ecstasy that a person can ever experience in life.

Yet marriage also can be, and frequently is, one of the most agonizing and excruciatingly painful events in the entire lifetime of many people. It can be an exasperating march through the exacerbating pains of the dungeons of hell on earth.

Few things in human conduct evoke such deep passion and pathos as the love between a man and a woman. These male-female relationships motivated by love, which we call marriage and divorce, constitute the basic foundation and structure of the family, and as such are of great importance to the state and to society.

We live in a rapidly changing world, and as the mores of the people change, the laws must change to accommodate their needs and desires. During the past 10 to 12 years, there have been some dramatic changes in the laws governing the male-female relationship once known as marriage, but now also known as cohabitation. The cohabiting arrangements discussed in Chapter 7 motivated the courts to try to change the laws to accommodate the new arrangements (the Marvin and Hewitt cases, for example), and it motivated legislatures to try to change the statutes to alleviate the revolt against the old-fashioned marriage and divorce laws. This chapter discusses these moving changes in the laws, and tells you how to use them.

HOW TO HANDLE YOUR OWN NO-FAULT DIVORCE

You have a legal right to represent yourself in court, as was discussed in Chapter 1.

The Georgia Constitution, Article 1, Section 1, provides:

No person shall be deprived of the right to prosecute or defend his own cause in any of the courts of this State, in person, by attorney, or both.

All states, by statute, constitutional provision, case law, or otherwise, give you the legal right to represent yourself in court. In Faretta v. California,[2] the U.S. Supreme Court said:

In the federal courts, the right of self-representation has been protected by statute since the beginnings of our Nation. Section 35 of the Judiciary Act of 1789, 1 Stat. 73, 92, enacted by the First Congress and signed by President Washington one day before the Sixth Amendment was proposed, provided that "in all the courts of the United States the parties may plead and manage their own causes personally or by the assistance of . . . counsel . . ." The right is currently codified in 28 U.S.C. Sec 1654.

One of the dissenting judges in the Faretta case said:

If there is any truth to the old proverb that "one who is his own lawyer has a fool for a client," the court by its opinion today now bestows a constitutional right on one to make a fool of himself.

Another judge said:

Pro se representation may at times serve the ideal of a fair trial better than representation by an attorney.[3]

In an annotation in American Law Reports,[4] the following statement is made:

The cases herein are in substantial agreement with the general proposition that a party in a civil action may appear either pro se or through counsel (pursuant to statute in some in-

---

[2]Faretta v. California, 422 U.S. 806
[3]U.S. ex rel Soto v. U.S., 504, F. 2d. 1339
[4]67 A.L.R., Second 1103

stances), but that he has no absolute right to do both in the absence of express statutory or constitutional provision.

The fact that you have a legal right to represent yourself in court does not mean that you should always dispense with the services of a lawyer. There are some cases in which you should represent yourself, and some cases in which you should not represent yourself.

WHEN YOU CAN REPRESENT YOURSELF

In any case that merely involves an uncontested no-fault divorce — without any disputes or controversies over property rights, alimony, support, custody, and the like — you can, and indeed should, represent yourself. It takes very little research and inquiry to learn how to fill in the blanks in a form, arrange for the service of a summons (if necessary), arrange for a hearing, and prepare your testimony. In fact, some people are embarrassed to have to pay a lawyer a fee when they learn how easy and uncomplicated the proceedings are. I have known some lawyers who were honest enough to admit that they were embarrassed to take substantial fees for handling no-fault divorce cases.

In most states, the proceedings are no more complicated than going down to the clerk to get a marriage license. Did you ever think of hiring a lawyer to get a marriage license? It is virtually the same thing! In fact, some states have already adopted procedures in which lawyers are not needed in certain divorce cases. You might think it is hard work to do the necessary research yourself; however, you will be pleased to learn how easy it is, and once you get started, it will be fun.

Typically, there are two situations in uncontested no-fault divorce proceedings in which you can easily handle all the legal proceedings yourself. The first is where one spouse is absent — usually out of the state — and the marriage relationship has ended. The second is where both spouses are in the state, both agree that a divorce is appropriate, and both agree to an amicable settlement of all property rights and other matters. In this second situation, you do not have to worry about getting the service of summons on the other party. In the first situation, the filing of forms and papers to get the service of summons might be the most difficult part for you.

Even in a contested case, if you and your spouse can work out some satisfactory settlement of all disputed matters and reduce your settlement to a written document, you can represent yourself and save a great deal of money, time, potential embarrassment, intimidation by lawyers, and frustration. You also can effectively represent yourself in court where your adversary hires a lawyer in a disputed case; however, if the litigation gets to the stage at which you cannot reach an amicable settlement, you should consider the advisability of employing a competent lawyer to help protect your interests.

RESEARCHING THE DIVORCE PROCESS

The first thing you should do is to go to the office of the clerk where divorce cases are filed. Make sure that you have the right court for these cases. Check out several divorce files and examine them carefully. These files are open to the general public, and you should have no difficulty in finding examples of just about every step you will need to take. The file index usually shows which cases concern divorce. If you need assistance, you can ask the clerk. You will immediately notice that, in most courts, the majority of the cases are handled by just a few lawyers in town; these are the divorce "specialists." Make notes on the names and addresses of these lawyers just in case you ever need one of them. If you must use a lawyer, it is always wise to hire one who has experience in handling divorce cases.

In reviewing the files, you should make notes on the kinds of pleadings that are filed, and learn how to prepare notices, briefs, orders, or other pleadings that might become necessary. You will notice that most of the cases fall into one of the following five categories:

- Uncontested with both parties signing the petition
- Uncontested "default" cases where one party fails to plead in the litigation
- Uncontested cases with settlement agreement signed by both parties
- Uncontested cases with no settlement agreement
- Contested cases

In practically all these situations, the main requirements are to:

- File the right papers to effect service of summons, if needed
- Prepare a settlement agreement
- Arrange for a hearing for the brief taking of testimony to the effect that the marriage is irretrievably broken (or other statutory language for no fault divorces)

After you review some of the court files and make notes on the pleadings, briefs, and other items of interest, you should arrange to get a copy of your state statutes on divorces. You also should obtain a copy of your court rules of civil procedure and a copy of any local court rules. Make sure you have all rules of court before you start. When you get a copy of the state statutes, make arrangements to obtain access to the *annotations* to the statutes — cases in your state that interpret and construe your state statutes. These are available in almost any law office or law library. Generally, you can learn more from a review of the court files and the briefs of lawyers than you can from personal research; however, you should be familiar with all cases on the main parts of the statutes.

When you have completed the review of the court files, done your legal research, obtained copies of the necessary materials, including the court rules, and talked with court personnel, you are ready to determine whether you should handle your case yourself. If you feel confortable about handling your own case and are reasonably sure you can complete all the steps required, you will enjoy being able to do it yourself. If, however, you feel insecure or uncertain about it, you should consider the advisability of obtaining help from a lawyer.

One of the most important aspects of hiring a lawyer in domestic cases is to be able to control your lawyer. It is very easy for lawyers to complicate very simple transactions. Make sure you do your own research and investigation so you can direct the litigation even if you use a good trial lawyer. Keep in mind, though, that about 90 percent of all the divorce cases handled by lawyers are settled out of court. The odds are quite good that you can settle your own case if you do not let emotions override your logic.

Chapter 14

Crimes, Criminals, and Criminal Law

The do-it-yourself concept works well in many areas of the law, and you can do most of your own legal work yourself in some areas of law without a lawyer. However, in criminal cases where your liberty and freedom may be in jeopardy, you will need professional help. In a criminal case, you will need all the help you can get. This chapter is designed to tell you your legal rights and how to protect them.

First, you should study, learn, and fully understand your constitutional and statutory rights in criminal matters. Second, you should be prepared to exercise and protect all your rights in the event you are charged with a crime. In exercising those rights, the first priority in most cases is to exercise your right to remain silent until you get adequate representation by a competent lawyer. You still can do a great deal of your own legal work in criminal cases, but you should have the help of your attorney.

To properly exercise your rights, you need to know more about your legal rights in the investigative, custodial, and interrogative phases of a case than you can learn from watching television. Your legal rights before you get an attorney and your right to the services of an attorney are critical. All phases of your case should be handled with the advice of your attorney. In a criminal case, you not only need a competent lawyer in whom you have confidence, but you need to follow your lawyer's advice.

WHAT IS A CRIME?

A *crime* is an offense against the state or sovereignty. It is an act committed, or omitted, in violation of a public law forbidding, or commanding, it. A crime is a wrong that the government claims is injurious to the public at large and punishes through a judicial proceeding in the name of the state. Although the same act might constitute both a crime and a *tort*, a crime is an offense against the public, while a tort is a private injury, which might result in the injured party bringing a lawsuit in a civil court for the recovery of damages.

Legal mental capacity to commit a crime is an essential prerequisite to criminal responsibility. Stated another way, an incompetent (insane) person is not capable of committing a crime.

At common law, a crime required two elements: an act, and an evil intention. Under the common law, proof of criminal intent is a necessary element in the prosecution of every criminal case, except those offenses that are merely *malum prohibitum,* that is, crimes in which a wrongful intent is presumed solely from the commission of the act itself.

The law has long divided crimes into acts wrong in themselves, called acts *mala in se,* and acts that would not be wrong but for the fact that positive law forbids them, called acts *mala prohibita.* An act that is *mala in se* is one inherently wicked, one naturally evil, as adjudged by the sense of a civilized community. It is one involving illegality from the very nature of the transaction, upon principles of natural, moral, and public law, and one immoral in its nature and injurious in its consequences, without regard to the fact of its being noticed or punished by the law of the state.

A *criminal motive* is that which leads or tempts the mind to indulge in a criminal act. It is the moving power that impels to action for a definite result. *Malice* is that state of mind which prompts the intentional doing of a wrongful act without legal justification or excuse. *Willful* denotes an act that is intentional, knowing, or voluntary, as distinguished from accidental.

Ordinarily you are not guilty of a crime unless you are aware of the existence of all the facts that make your conduct criminal, but there are some exceptions to this rule. For example, voluntary intoxication or narcosis (drugs) is generally not a good defense to an unlawful act committed while "under the influence."

The word *criminal* denotes one who has committed an offense, one who has been legally convicted of a crime, or one, who has been adjudged guilty of a crime. The adjective *criminal* denotes that which pertains to or is connected with the law of crimes or the administration of penal justice, or which relates to or has the character of crime. *Criminal procedure* is that set of rules administered by the criminal courts in the administration of the criminal system of justice.

LEGAL RIGHTS OF U.S. CITIZENS

I have, from time to time, asserted that our federal government intrudes itself into our daily lives too much. By way of the "confessions of a mad lawyer," however, I must admit that the federal government has come through with flying colors when we consider the individual rights of citizens of the United States, as compared with those of other countries, in criminal matters.

The United States Constitution, especially the Bill of Rights and the several amendments, and as interpreted by the Warren court in a series of decisions by the U.S. Supreme Court, forms the legal foundation for a wide range of protection for citizens charged with a crime. On balance and from an historical and philosophical point of view, it is good. Tyranny in the pursuit of justice is not all bad.

The limitation of space does not permit a detailed discussion of each of the important criminal decisions of the U.S. Supreme Court. A few, however, will be discussed briefly.

Rarely do people plan for future criminal proceedings in their personal lives, but it is very important for you to know your legal rights just in case you should be charged with a crime. Knowing your rights is especially important if you are falsely charged, or if you get in a position where your lack of knowledge about your legal rights might result in your waiving them.

Do not be bashful in demanding your constitutional rights, including the Fifth Amendment. It is an absolute right we all have. The following is only a partial list of your most fundamental rights:

- Freedom of speech
- Freedom of the press
- Freedom of assembly

- Freedom of religion
- Right to vote
- Right to hold office
- Right to keep and bear arms
- Right to individual privacy
- Right to full enjoyment of your property
- Right to equal protection of the laws
- Right to privilege against self-incrimination
- Right to due process of law
- Right to habeas corpus
- Right against double jeopardy
- Right to a jury trial

Most of us learned about these rights in school, but many American citizens soon forget them. Although they are all very important, I want to discuss briefly how to apply these rules when you need them.

The U.S. Supreme Court, in a series of leading cases, has clearly defined some of the rights we have under the United States Constitution and its amendments. The Fourth Amendment provides:

The right to the people to be secure in their persons, houses, papers, and effects, against unreasonable searches and seizures, shall not be violated, and no Warrants shall issue but upon probable cause, supported by Oath or affirmation, and particularly describing the place to be searched, and the persons or things to be seized.

The Fifth Amendment provides:

No person shall be held to answer for a capital, or otherwise infamous crime, unless on a presentment or indictment of a grand jury, except in cases arising in the land or Naval forces, or in the Militia, when in actual service in time of War or public danger; nor shall any person be subject for the same offence to be twice put in jeopardy of life or limb; nor shall be compelled in any criminal case, to be a witness against himself, nor be deprived of life, liberty, or property, without due process of law; nor shall private property be taken for public use without just compensation.

The Fourth Amendment to the Constitution was a reaction to the evils of the use of the general warrant in England and the writs of assistance in the Colonies, and was intended to protect against invasions of the sanctity of a person's home and the privacies of life from searches under indiscriminate, general authority.

It is apparent that the problems which might be confronted in a search and seizure case are myriad and complex; however, the case can be approached with four basic questions:

- Was there a "search" or "seizure" within the meaning of the Fourth Amendment?
- Was a warrant (a) required, and (b) obtained?
- Was the warrant valid?
- Was the search or seizure properly conducted and properly limited in scope?

The Fourth Amendment does not forbid all searches and seizures, only *unreasonable searches and seizures*. Sufficient probability, not certainty, is the touchstone of reasonableness under the Fourth Amendment. Reasonableness is to be determined in the light of the total atmosphere of the case. In the area of reasonableness of search and seizure, each case must be judged on its own particular facts and circumstances.

It has been said that the law of searches and seizures under the Fourth and Fifth amendments to the U.S. Constitution reflects a dual purpose:

- Protection of the privacy of the individual, that is, of his right to be let alone
- Protection of the individual against compulsory production of evidence to be used against him

The overriding function of the Fourth Amendment is to protect personal privacy and dignity against unwarranted intrusion by the state. The basic purpose of the Fourth Amendment is to safeguard the privacy and security of individuals against arbitrary invasions by governmental officials. The amendment thus gives concrete expression to a right of the people that is basic to a free society.

Chief Justice Earl Warren delivered the opinion of the U.S. Supreme Court in the now famous *Miranda* decision, in which the issue before the court was stated as follows:

> The cases before us raise questions which go to the roots of our concepts of American criminal jurisprudence: the restraints society must observe consistent with the Federal Constitution in prosecuting individuals for crime. More specifically, we deal with the admisability of statements obtained from an individual who is subjected to custodial police interrogation and the necessity for procedures which assure that the individual is accorded his privilege under the Fifth Amendment to the Constitution not to be compelled to incriminate himself.

The holding of the Court was as follows:

> Our holding will be spelled out with some specificity in the pages which follow but briefly stated it is this: the prosecution may not use statements, whether exculpatory or inculpatory, stemming from custodial interrogation of the defendant unless it demonstrates the use of procedural safeguards effective to secure the privilege against self-incrimination. By custodial interrogation, we mean questioning initiated by law enforcement officers after a person has been taken into custody or otherwise deprived of his freedom of action in any significant way. As for the procedural safeguards to be employed, unless other fully effective means are devised to inform accused persons of their right of silence and to assure a continuous opportunity to exercise it, the following measures are required. Prior to any questioning, the person must be warned that he has a right to remain silent, that any statement he does make may be used as evidence against him, and that he has a right to the presence of an attorney, either retained or appointed. The defendant may waive effectuation of these rights, provided the waiver is made voluntarily, knowingly and intelligently. If, however, he indicates in any manner and at any stage of the process that he wishes to consult with an attorney before speaking there can be no questioning. LIkewise, if the individual is alone and indicates in any manner that he does not wish to be interrogated, the police may not question him. The mere fact that he may have

answered some questions or volunteered some statements on his own does not deprive him of the right to refrain from answering any further inquiries until he has consulted with an attorney and thereafter consents to be questioned.

In the case of *Gideon v. Wainwright,* the Supreme Court held that a state court, on request of an indigent defendant in a case involving a serious crime, must appoint counsel for him, and must grant the request without considering whether the defendant's trial without counsel would, under the particular circumstances shown, involve such a lack of essential fairness as to constitute a violation of the due process requirements of the Fourteenth Amendment. The Court held that the *assistance of counsel* clause in the Sixth Amendment is made obligatory on the states by virtue of the Fourteenth Amendment.

Although all these rights are of great importance, always remember that you should, in a criminal case, make assistance of counsel the absolute first priority.

YOUR LEGAL RIGHT TO REPRESENT YOURSELF IN COURT

Notwithstanding the suggestions made earlier about obtaining the services of an attorney, you do have a legal right to represent yourself in court, to be your own lawyer, if you wish to do so. You should be very careful, however, in exercising this right. Where substantial property rights or serious crimes are involved, you should always consider the services of a good lawyer. In small civil cases and minor criminal matters, such as traffic violations, you might be able to represent yourself. You especially might want to represent yourself in small cases, where you frequently pay more in attorney's fees than the whole case is worth.

The "free" lawyers provided by the state in criminal matters aren't all as good as Perry Mason. Many of them are among the large percentage of lawyers in this country whom the Chief Justice of the United States has said are incompetent to handle trials. Just be careful to get a good, competent, experienced lawyer if you can.

A federal statute[1] provides:

---

[1] 28 U.S.C. 1654

139

In all courts of the United States the parties may plead and conduct their own cases personally or by counsel as, by the rules of such courts, respectively, are permitted to manage and conduct causes therein.

The constitutions and statutes of many states have a similar provision.

As you have seen, you have a constitutional right to a lawyer in criminal cases. What happens, though, if the state provides you with a lawyer and you do not want him? Can the court force a lawyer upon you? No!

The U.S. Supreme Court has held:

The Sixth and Fourteenth Amendments of our Constitution guarantee that a person brought to trial in any state or federal court must be afforded the right to the assistance of counsel before he can be validly convicted and punished by imprisonment. This clear constitutional rule has emerged from a series of cases decided here over the last 50 years. The question before us now is whether a defendant in a state criminal trial has a constitutional right to proceed *without* counsel when he voluntarily and intelligently elects to do so. Stated another way, the question is whether a State may constitutionally hale a person into its criminal courts and there force a lawyer upon him, even when he insists that he wants to conduct his own defense. It is not an easy question, but we have concluded that a State may not constitutionally do so.[2]

With all their defects, most courts in this country, both criminal and civil, are far superior to those of most countries, except perhaps England and Canada. Despite all the criticism of lawyers, many lawyers in this country are superior in their dedication to service even though they must charge high fees. You can improve your position greatly if you realize that all lawyers are not qualified to handle all kinds of cases, and approach the selection of a lawyer with care and with an investigative attitude. You can save on legal fees by doing some legal research yourself. Moreover, you might wish to plan ahead by getting prepaid legal services.

---

[2]Faretta v. California, 422 U.S. 806) (1975)

Chapter 15

What Happens If
You Get Arrested?

If you should ever be accused of, charged with, or arrested for a crime, it will be too late to try to look at some legal manual to discover your rights and to learn what you should do to protect your rights. You should review these steps carefully and understand all your rights because they could be of critical importance if you ever have the full force and power of the state against you.

When a person gets arrested, there is usually an immediate search for evidence. As a general rule, if you are charged with a serious crime, you should not give any evidence to the law enforcement authorities without competent advice from a lawyer who knows enough about the case to form an intelligent judgment.

Every citizen of the United States has the following rights, among others:

- In making an arrest, the police must inform the accused of his rights and give him an opportunity to telephone a relative, friend, or lawyer.
- The accused has the right to a lawyer's services from the moment of arrest, and need not say anything until he consults with his lawyer.
- He has a right to know the charges against him.
- He has a right to a reasonably prompt hearing before a magistrate.

- If held for trial, the accused has a right to have reasonable bail set as security for his release, except for certain major crimes or at the discretion of the court.
- He has a right to speedy trial.
- He has a right to confront and cross-examine his accusers and to call witnesses on his own behalf.
- He cannot be tried twice for the same offense.
- If he is convicted, he cannot be subjected to cruel and unusual punishment.

An accused may knowingly waive these rights, but it is foolish to do so. In summary: don't talk until you get a lawyer.

When you do obtain the services of an attorney, you should be prepared to give him pertinent information that will help in your defense. The things you should be prepared to give your attorney include the following:

- Facts of the case, including details of the alleged crime
- Names and addresses of persons who might be witnesses to the facts of the crime
- Prior criminal record, if any
- Employment record
- Persons who could be used as character witnesses
- Persons who could testify to an alibi, if applicable
- Relatives and friends who could assist in obtaining bail
- Personal business that must be completed during the period you are in jail awaiting the posting of bail
- Details of the arrest

PRELIMINARY HEARINGS

The accused is generally entitled to have a preliminary hearing on any charges against him within a reasonable time after arrest. At this hearing, the state is required to establish that a crime was committed and that there is reasonable and proper cause to believe the accused committed the crime charged. It is not necessary at this time for the state to prove its accusations beyond reasonable doubt.

At the preliminary hearing, the defense attorney has the right to cross-examine the witnesses called by the state, although he has no obligation to call witnesses on the defendant's case. In some cases, however, the attorney for the accused might want to call witnesses on his case in order to preserve testimony of witnesses who might leave the jurisdiction or die, or to otherwise establish testimony for use later. In some states, the defense of insanity and alibi should be raised at the preliminary hearing if they are to be relied on by the defendant. If a confession or admission of the defendant is used by the prosecution and the defendant contends that it was extracted by force, the validity and propriety of the confession should be raised at the earliest possible time. Where the defendant fails to raise these issues at the earliest possible time, that failure subsequently might be used against him in the determination of the propriety of the confession.

At the preliminary hearing or, subsequently, at the arraignment, the defendant will have an opportunity to object to any illegal search or seizure. If the defendant's premises have been searched in violation of his constitutional rights or his person has been searched, except as an incident to an otherwise legal arrest, the evidence thus obtained may not be admissible. In some states if the defendant was aware of the illegal search, he must raise the issue prior to trial or it might be waived.

The validity of the arrest also can be determined at the preliminary hearing, if it is at issue. In most states, the powers of the peace officer or a citizen to make an arrest are spelled out by statute. The rules relating to the validity of an arrest might vary depending on the crime charged.

GRAND JURY

If the defendant is accused of a felony, the case generally will be submitted to a grand jury. The grand jury is required to inquire into crimes and make accusations in accordance with the law.

To find an indictment, the grand jury must rely on *legal evidence,* that is, sworn testimony, depositions, and documentary proof. The evidence presented need only make out a *prima facie* case; that is, every element of the crime must be established. Generally, the crime will be established in broad terms before the grand jury, leaving details to be established later at the trial.

In some cases, the defendant may volunteer to appear before the grand jury, but he will not have a right to do so unless it is specifically provided by statute. Where the defendant appears before the grand jury, it is usually without counsel, and after the defendant has agreed to waive immunity.

In most states, the grand jury is not limited to investigating and returning indictments concerning defendants already in custody. In its discretion, the grand jury also can undertake broad investigations.

Generally, the defendant in a criminal case might have the right to refuse to testify before a grand jury if he has been accused of a crime or if the testimony would tend to incriminate him. Where the defendant does not have the right to refuse to testify, he will have the right to refuse to answer specific questions if his answer would incriminate him. Although the court must be the final judge of whether a question will incriminate the defendant, lack of knowledge generally forces the court to rely upon the defendant for the determination. It would not be proper to ask the defendant why he was invoking the privilege afforded by the Fifth Amendment.

An accused will not be permitted to avail himself of his constitutional right against self-incrimination where he has been granted immunity. In many jurisdictions, the immunity will be applicable only to prosecutions in that jurisdiction. Similarly, a defendant will not be excused from answering questions if the answer would tend to incriminate him with respect to a crime for which the statute of limitations has run out or if the answer would merely tend to subject the defendant to civil liability.

The grand jury will either render an indictment against the defendant or refuse to render an indictment. Where the grand jury renders the indictment, the defendant will be arraigned.

ARRAIGNMENT

The arraignment to the charge or to the indictment gives the defendant an opportunity to hear the indictment rendered by the grand jury. The reading of the indictment can be dispensed with where the defendant has been provided with a copy prior to the arraignment.

In some cases, the defendant's attorney and the prosecutor's office will discuss, prior to the arraignment, the charge and the pleas that the defendant will enter. In settling a criminal case, the defendant might agree to plead guilty to a lesser charge, thereby eliminating the need for trial. A great majority of criminal cases are settled before trial. In many cases, however, a criminal case will be more difficult to settle than a civil case because of the influence of intensive public attention, political pressures, or the defendant's refusal to plead guilty to any charge.

Where a plea is being worked out, it might be possible to obtain a commitment from the judge as to the sentence that will be imposed. If the judge will not commit himself in advance, it might be necessary to rely on experience with a particular judge in sentencing, or the statutory maximum and minimum sentence for the crime charged. Where sentencing has been discussed with the court prior to entering pleas for several crimes, counsel should determine whether the sentences to be imposed by the court will run concurrently or consecutively.

MOTIONS

Although your attorney will be handling most of the legal proceedings, it is important for you to know and understand these proceedings. Generally, motions during the preliminary proceedings include the following:

- Bill of Particulars
- Motions to Inspect the Minutes of the Grand Jury
- Motions to Quash, Dismiss or Set Aside the Indictment
- A Demurrer

In most areas of the nation, most defendants will exhaust all plea bargaining before trial. Prosecuting attorneys are notoriously overworked, they say, and it is frequently common practice for defendants to be able to get off with a lesser charge, thereby avoiding a trial.

Every defendant is entitled to a fair trial, by jury in most cases. He also may appeal any verdict or judgment rendered against him.

Chapter 16

Small Claims Court

The development of small claims courts in the United States is the result of reformist activity at the beginning of this century. The reformers, among them some of the most outstanding legal scholars of their day, were particularly interested in relieving the legal and monetary difficulties experienced by less affluent litigants and other individuals with a valid, but small, monetary claim. In some states, these people could turn to the justice of the peace courts, but these tribunals were confined to certain areas and were notorious for the low quality of justice they provided. Thus, no legal institution existed to deal adequately with small claims at that time.

One of the early advocates of the small claims courts was Dean Roscoe Pound, who said:

It is here that the administration of justice touches immediately the greatest number of people. It is here that the great mass of an urban population, whose experience of the law in the past has been too often experience only of the arbitrary discretion of police officers, might be made to feel that the law is a living force for securing their individual as well as their collective interests. For there is a strong social interest in the moral and social life of the individual. If the will of the individual is subjected arbitrarily to the will of others because the means of protection are too cumbrous and expensive to be available for one of his means or the inclination to resist, there is an injury to society at large.[1]

The general purpose of small claims courts is to provide a summary procedure for the litigation of small claims, that is, claims not exceeding a certain specified amount — usually $1000 to $5000. Therefore, certain legal technicalities that might encumber an ordinary proceeding are generally dispensed with in a small claims proceeding. The substantive law applicable in a small claims proceeding is, however, the same as that applicable in a regular proceeding.

Typical of the court rules in small claims courts is that of New York, which provides:

The court shall conduct hearings upon small claims in such manner as to do substantial justice between the parties according to the rules of substantive law and shall not be bound by statutory provisions or rules of practice, procedure, pleading or evidence.[2]

This is, of course, a perfectly reasonable provision because cases involving very complicated legal issues can and should be transferred to the regular civil courts.

The formal rules of evidence should not apply to small claims procedures. The report of the National Institute for Consumer Justice states that a court attempting to force adherence by all small claims litigants to the rules of evidence would have no time to devote to the substance of the cases before it. Because of the relative informality of most consumer transactions, the majority of consumers do not receive or retain the evidence necessary to conform to the formal rules of evidence. In response to this reality, a Philadelphia small claims court rule provides:

When a claim is based upon a written contract, three copies of at least pertinent portions must be filed with the statement

---

[1]Pound, Dean Roscoe, "The Administration of Justice in the Modern City," *Harvard Law Review*, 1913, 26:302.

[2]New York Civil Court Act, Article 18, Section 1804, McKinney Supp., 1972.

of claim. However, if the contract is not available, it is sufficient simply to explain why and describe its provisions.[3]

One difficulty faced by many consumer plaintiffs in recent years has been discovering the official legal name of the firm they wish to sue. This often involves intensive research into the files at municipal or state offices. The problem should be resolved by allowing suits to be brought in the name listed on the defendant's business premises, letterheads, or advertisements. Many courts already have implemented this practice.

You need not retain a lawyer to sue in small claims court. In fact, some courts do not permit attorneys. Court filing fees usually range from $2 to $15, and judgment in your favor as a rule includes recovery of filing fees. You may state your grievance in plain words; you do not need to know a lot of legal jargon. In most small claims courts, the judge will not insist on formal procedures or strict rules of evidence. You tell your side of the story, and the other party tells his side. Cases come to trial, as a rule, without the long delays so common in most civil courts. Decisions usually are rendered immediately from the bench, or within a few days after trial.

Almost every state has some kind of small claims court. The most you can claim is usually $5,000, and in some courts somewhat more. The trend is to higher limits in such courts. In some cases, the defendant may have a case removed to a higher civil court where the proceedings are more formal. Either way, you can handle it yourself.

Small claims courts are often called by other names, for example, justice court, district court, municipal court, justice of the peace, county court, civil court, magistrate's court, court of record, conciliation court, circuit court, court of common pleas, and others.

HOW TO GET A CASE STARTED

Ask the court clerk whether the court can handle your kind of case. Get a copy of the court rules, if any. Most courts have jurisdiction over contractual disputes — the usual run of buyer-seller controversies involving money damages — and claims of damages through negligence, such as auto accident claims.

---

[3]Philadelphia Municipal Court Civil Procedure Rule 107(e) 1971

Some large cities have special courts that handle landlord-tenant disputes.

You also can ask the clerk whether the court has jurisdiction over the party you wish to sue, but do not necessarily accept his word as final. The usual rule is that a defendant must live, work, or do business in the court's territory. Complications might arise with out-of-town firms. You might have to file suit in the defendant's city or county instead of your own. This is the jurisdiction-venue problem. With an out-of-state firm, you might need to contact your state government (usually the secretary of state) to find out where to make service of process. If a firm does business in your state, they can be sued in your state. The clerk can help you in serving process. The success of your action also might hinge on whether the firm you sue is still in business and whether you can make the defendant pay a judgment. Do not waste a lot of time in litigation unless you are fairly sure you will be able to collect your judgment.

Double-check the business name and address of the company you are suing. In some courts, the suit might be dismissed unless you have identified the company exactly as it has registered itself for legal purposes. Ask the clerk whether strict accuracy is required, and, if so, how to find the correct name and address.

A good source of information about how to proceed in small claims court are people who already have been through the proceedings. If you have the time, you should watch a session of the court in action before your own case comes to trial.

Prepare for trial by gathering all pertinent receipts, canceled checks, contracts, bills, purchase orders, written estimates, pictures, and other documentary evidence. Set down the events in chronological order, and check the dates carefully. Arrange for all witnesses you might need to attend the trial and testify.

In disputes over workmanship, a disinterested person in the same trade makes an ideal witness. If he will not appear in person, his written statement might be viewed as acceptable evidence in court. Not all courts accept such statements, however. Check with the clerk on this point. Bring to court the physical evidence of your claim, such as clothing ruined by the dry cleaner whom you are suing, or a defective appliance, or any other exhibit or object you think will support your side of the case.

If your opponent offers to settle out of court, have him put it down in written form. File a copy signed by both parties with the court so that the agreement can be enforced by law. You also can ask him to appear with you in court to tell the judge the settlement terms and have them recorded by the judge. Always try to collect your court costs if possible. The court usually will award you the court costs if you win the case.

The most important thing to do in preparing for the trial is to know the date, time, and place of your trial, and to be there on time. You should notify the clerk if you and the defendant settle your claim before the date set for trial.

If you are the defendant and you do not wish to contest the plaintiff's claim, you may settle with him before the date set for trial and have the action dismissed by the court. If you do not settle and do not appear at the trial, a judgment might be awarded against you by default. You may answer the complaint, stating your defenses, and you also may file a counterclaim against the plaintiff for any claims you have against him. The clerk can explain the counterclaim procedures to you and usually provide appropriate forms to use.

Remember: Whether you are the plaintiff or the defendant, you must appear at trial, or you might lose the case automatically. If there is some important reason why you cannot be in court on the day of your trial, call the court clerk and try to arrange for a continuance of the trial to another date.

WHAT TO DO AT TRIAL

The trial is just a simple, informal hearing before the judge or a referee. Try to get to court early so you will have time to find the small claims courtroom, but remember, there might be a number of cases to be heard so you will need to wait your turn. Waiting will give you an opportunity to see how the court procedures work.

If the person you are suing does not appear for the trial and he was properly served with the notice, then you probably will win your suit by default, but you might have to explain your case to the judge. If the defendant does appear, then the judge will hold a hearing and decide which of the parties should win the case. If you are the defendant and the plaintiff does not appear for the trial, the suit against you usually will be dismissed.

When your case is called, you should try to explain as simply as possible why the person you are suing owes you money. Be sure to offer all your evidence and witnesses. If you are the defendant, you will have an opportunity to explain why you do not owe the plaintiff the money for which he is suing. The judge might help both parties by asking questions, and you should try to answer these questions clearly and directly. There are usually a large number of small claims cases to be heard, and you have a limited time to present your case. Always have a written outline of all of your points, and make sure they are all covered.

GETTING YOUR MONEY AFTER YOU WIN

If the court decides in your favor, a formal judgment or court order will be entered. After you get the judgment, you should make demand on the defendant to pay you immediately. If he refuses to pay you the money after you have received a judgment, you then should obtain a writ of execution or garnishment from the court clerk and have it served to seize any of the defendant's property or assets you can find. The court cannot collect your money for you, so you need to be an investigator and locate the assets of the defendant yourself.

Chapter 17

How To Form
Your Own Corporation

Most large companies have a corporate legal staff with specialists in various fields to keep the company current on the numerous and constantly changing laws. Inflation has driven private legal counsel out of reach of many owners of small businesses, however, there are many legal problems you can solve yourself. Forming your own corporation without a lawyer is easy. You will be surprised and delighted to learn how easy it is to form your own corporation in your own state, and you will be especially pleased to learn how inexpensive it is.

In this chapter, you will learn the advantages and disadvantages of the corporate form of business as compared with others. You will discover the dangers of forming a "foreign" corporation (the so-called *Delaware corporation*), its excessive costs, the hidden legal liabilities, and the realization that once you form a foreign corporation, you cannot legally do business in your own state without registering your foreign corporation in your state. The additional costs associated with the foreign corporation make it even less desirable.

Once you decide to incorporate in your home state, simply follow the step-by-step instructions outlined here to accomplish it.

Legal fees for having an attorney file your incorporation papers run from $500 to $2,000 or more. I do not mean to imply that these fees are excessive. Indeed, incorporation is an important step in your business career. Yet, if you learn how to do it yourself, you can save a substantial amount of money. If you do need legal advice about any aspect of the transaction, the information in this chapter will enable you to ask your lawyer the right questions and enable you to understand the answers better.

I will summarize the laws governing corporations, and include a list of the forms and other documents you will need. I will not, however, give specific legal advice on specific fact situations.

The primary objectives of this chapter are to explore the factors you need to consider in determining whether you should incorporate; to give you the procedures and laws applicable to the creation, organization, and operation of a corporation as a business entity; to enable you to determine whether, where, and under what circumstances you should incorporate; and to explain how you can form your own corporation under the laws of your state.

You are not legally required to have a lawyer to form your corporation and start your own business. In complex corporate transactions, however, you might need professional advice and counsel.

TYPES OF CORPORATIONS

A *corporation* is "an artificial being, invisible, intangible, and existing only in contemplation of law."[1] Another legal definition of a corporation is:

A corporation may be described as being an artificial being, existing only in contemplation of law; a legal entity, a fictitious person, vested by law with the capacity of taking and granting property and transacting business as an individual. It is composed of a number of individuals, authorized to act as if they were one person. The individual stockholders are the constituents or component parts through whose intelligence, judgment, and discretion the corporation acts. The affairs of a corporation cannot in many cases be conveniently conducted and managed by the stockholders, for they are often numerous and widely separated; yet they, in reality, compose the body corporate.[2]

[1]Dartmouth College v. Woodward, 4 Wheat, 518, 4 L. Ed. 629
[2]Jones v. Williams, et al, 139 Mo. 1, 39 S.W. 486, 490 (1897)

A corporation is a separate thing, an artificial person or legal entity that you can create by following the steps set out in the statutes of your state. These legal definitions are correct descriptions of a corporation; however, it is within the power of your state legislature to define a corporation. If an association falls within that definition, the courts will recognize it as legally binding. The most important thing for you to know is that a corporation is a separate, distinct entity from you, even though you might own substantially all of the stock and conduct most of the activities of the corporation.

Corporations fall into the following broad classifications:

- Public
- Quasi-public
- Private or profit-making
- Nonprofit
- Foreign
- Domestic

A *public corporation* is one created for public purposes only. It is connected with the administration of the government. Examples are states, school districts, cities, and counties. *Quasi-public* is a term applied to corporations that are not strictly public in the sense of being organized for governmental purposes. Quasi-public corporations are those that operate by contributing to the comfort, convenience, and welfare of the general public. Examples are gas, water, electric, and other utility companies.

Private corporations are created for private purposes, as distinguished from those purely public, and are generally thought of as business entities carrying on activities for profit-making purposes. A profit-making corporation is primarily a business corporation organized with a view toward gains that are to be distributed among its members. A *nonprofit corporation,* sometimes referred to as *eleemosynary,* is one created for or devoted to charitable purposes or those supported by charity.

A *foreign corporation* is one organized in another state or country. A *domestic corporation* is one organized within the state. It is not recommended that you organize your corporation in a foreign state or other jurisdiction.

The character of a corporation is determined by the object of its formation and the nature of its business. The character of a corporation may not be changed by calling it something different from that specified in its articles of incorporation. Because of this requirement, you should make certain that the articles sufficiently describe and define the purposes for which you are establishing the corporation.

CONSIDERATIONS

In considering whether or not to form a corporation, you should know the options that are available and their characteristics as compared to incorporation. Some of the most important items to consider in making a decision include:

- Liability exposure
- Tax costs and considerations
- Centralization of management
- Advantages of raising capital through issuance of stock
- Ability to attract and keep key personnel through various fringe benefits or participation as stockholders
- The practical convenience of the various forms in which a business might be conducted

As the risk of potential personal liability increases, whether from the nature of the business or from the extent of your assets, the value of eliminating personal liability increases and the advantage of the corporate form increases. The small expenses involved in setting up a corporation are relatively insignificant when compared with the liability factors.

Other forms of business entities include:

- Individual proprietorship
- Partnership
- Limited partnership
- Combination of partnership and corporation
- Multiple corporations

In deciding which form of business you wish to use, you should consider the following factors:

- Simplicity

- Organizational flexibility
- Financing
- Continuity
- Tranferability of shares
- Goodwill
- Compensation arrangements
- Fringe benefits
- Estate liquidity
- Splitting of income among family members

The following factors are considered the most significant reasons to adopt the corporate form of business entity:

- The owners, stockholders, or principals have no individual liability other than the capital contribution in stock payments.
- Corporations can be perpetual.
- Corporations are a separate entity from the stockholders. They can sue and be sued, and hold and deal in property.
- Stock can be sold or otherwise transferred at will.
- Corporations can raise capital by the insurance of new stock, bonds, or other securities.
- A board of directors is the center of authority, acting by a majority agreement.
- As a separate entity, a corporation has credit possibilities apart from stockholders, and stock is sometimes available as collateral.
- Corporations have flexibility in that the charter and bylaws can be changed easily.
- The trend in the business world is toward greater use of the corporation. This trend is a result of the ever increasing exposure to personal liability, the ease with which you can incorporate under the simplified state laws, and the other advantages of incorporation.
- The tax advantages of incorporation include the use of a corporation as a tax shelter; wealth-building advantages under corporate pension and profit-sharing plans; group life, medical, and hospital insurance coverage for owners; deductions for business losses; prepaid legal services; and others.

STEPS IN CREATING
AND ORGANIZING YOUR CORPORATION

Establishing your corporation is a simple matter once you determine the statutory requirements. The procedures are set out in each state statute. Most statutes, based on the Model Business Corporation Act, require nothing more than these simple steps:

- Selecting the corporate name
- Filling out a form of articles of incorporation, usually furnished by the secretary of state or another officer designated to administer corporations
- Filing the form with the filing fees
- Getting a corporate kit
- Holding an organizational meeting and preparing minutes of the meeting

The secretary of state can give you the necessary forms, or you can type the articles of incoporation. You can purchase a corporate kit, or you can make your own.

You can obtain a copy of your state's corporation statutes in any law library. In some states, the secretary of state has a summary of the corporate statutes you need for forming a corporation. A summary of each of the state statutes is contained in the *Martindale-Hubbell Law Directory,* found in most law libraries. You can call, write, or visit the state office that administers the corporation laws to obtain forms and information on filing fees. Your letter can be based on this sample:

TO THE SECRETARY OF STATE:

I wish to form a profit-making corporation in this state, and request that you send me any forms you have for effecting such incorporation, along with any information or instruction booklets you have. Also, please send me a schedule of your fees for incorporation.

Each state office has several people whose primary duties are to assist in filing these papers and to keep the corporate records of the state. They are usually helpful and cooperative in giving any information or assistance needed. The following list contains all of the steps necessary to complete your incorporation:

- Determine the availability of your corporate name
- File the articles of incorporation
- Pay filing fees
- Hold an organizational meeting and prepare minutes of the meeting
- Handle any local filings
- Prepare and approve bylaws
- Obtain a corporate kit

Most kits contain a corporate seal, stock register, stock certificate book, bylaws, and minutes book. You can purchase a kit at most large stationery stores, or you can prepare one yourself. Two companies that sell these kits are:

Excelsior-Legal (Order from the branch nearest you.)

62 White Street	P.O. Box 889
New York, NY 10013	Norcross, GA 30091
1 – 212 – 431 – 7000	1 – 404 – 449 – 5091
P.O. Box 4956	P.O. Box 5683
Chicago, IL 69680	Arlington, TX 76011
1 – 312 – 786 – 9528	1 – 817 – 461 – 5993

Corpex
Dept. A
480 Canal Street
New York, NY 10013

The prices range from $40 to $50 each. Both of these companies regularly advertise their kits in the *American Bar Association Journal,* which is available at most local libraries or from any lawyer's office.

If you decide to prepare your own corporate records, the forms at the end of this chapter will be useful.

LEGAL PRINCIPLES GOVERNING CORPORATIONS

For most purposes, a corporation is an entity distinct from its individual members or stockholders, who, as natural persons, are merged in the corporate entity. The corporation's identity remains unchanged and unaffected by changes in its individual membership. By the very nature of a corporation, its property is vested in the corporation itself and not the stockholders. The stockholders, as such, do not have the power to represent the corporation or act for it in relation to its ordinary business, nor are they personally liable for the acts and obligations of the corporation. In no legal sense can the business of a corporation be said to be that of its individual stockholders or officers.

The corporate entity is distinct even if all or a majority of its stock is owned by a single individual or corporation, or if the corporation is a so-called *closed,* or family, *corporation.* Thus, the ownership of all shares of stock of a corporation by one individual does not avoid the separate identity between the corporation and the individual.

No corporation can exist without the consent or grant of the sovereign, or the State. The power to create corporations is one of the attributes of sovereignty. This power is a legislative function. The laws, rules, regulations, and precedures for creating a corporation are established by the legislature through the enactment of statutes. Implementation of these procedures is a function of the executive branch of the state and is usually delegated to the office of the secretary of state or some other administrative officer. The federal government has power to create corporations, but those laws are not applicable to our discussions.

It is common for the general corporation laws of each state to provide for the formation of a corporation for any lawful business purpose or purposes. The forms normally have a blank space for stating the purpose for which a corporation is formed. In most states, only one person or another corporation can form a corporation. Some states require more than one incorporator.

The contents of the Articles of incorporation are determined by the local statutes. Most modern statutes, based on the Model Business Corporation Act, require the following items in the articles:

- Name of the corporation
- Period of duration
- Purpose or purposes for which the corporation is being organized

- Number, amount, description, and nature of shares of stock authorized
- Names and addresses of officers, directors, incorporators, and resident agent

Ordinarily, persons who combine their capital in a business venture are legally liable as partners unless they are protected by incorporation. The decisive question in determining personal liability is whether what has been done toward incorporation and organization is sufficient to constitute a corporation. If it is, then the individuals are not personally liable. Therefore, it is important for incorporators to fulfill the requirements of a valid corporation. Make sure you comply with all the requirements of your state's statute in forming your corporation.

A name is necessary to the very existence of a corporation. Each corporation must have a name by which it can be identified, function, and operate in the conduct of any legal acts or activities. The name of a corporation designates the corporation in the same manner as the name of an individual. The right to use its corporate name is one of the legal attributes of incorporation and constitutes a franchise or a privilege granted by the state. The presence or absence in a trade name of the word *company,* in and of itself, has no direct bearing on the issue as to whether the association is a corporation, partnership, or other entity.

Most statutes prohibit a private corporation from using the words *bank, insurance, trust,* and other names that might mislead the public. A corporation may adopt any name it desires, subject to the qualification that it cannot adopt or use a name already used by another corporation in the state. Corporations and unincorporated associations may have a property right in their names. A corporation cannot adopt a name so similar to that of another corporation, association, or firm that confusion or deception would result. It may not use its name for the purposes of pirating the business of a competitor. A corporation cannot adopt the name of an individual where it appears that the use of such a name would lead to confusion, deception to the public, or defrauding of others operating a business under the same name, even though the name was taken from the names of principal stockholders, promoters, or incorporators.

A corporation may use and adopt any seal or mark as its official corporate seal. Under the old common-law rules, a corporate seal was essential; however, this is no longer a legal requirement. In all business transactions and legal relationships where a natural person will be legally bound without a seal, a corporation also will be bound. For this reason, it is not necessary to obtain a corporate seal; however, a seal is usually one of the items included in the corporate kit. Even though the seal is not legally necessary, the presence of the corporate seal establishes, on its face, that the instrument to which it is affixed is the act of the corporation.

The governing structures of a corporation are its *bylaws*. They prescribe the rights and duties of its members; they establish the corporation's procedures, practices, and policies of business operation. Also, the bylaws contain the rules for the management of corporate affairs.

The *records* of a corporation include its articles of incorporation and bylaws, the minutes of its meetings, the stock books, the books containing the account of its official activities, and the written evidence of its contracts and business transactions.

A *share of stock* is a unit of interest in a corporation. Even though ownership of stock does not confer title to any of the property of the corporation, it legally entitles the shareholder to an equivalent part of the property, or its proceeds, when distributed. *Common stock* is the class of stock that is ordinarily issued without extraordinary rights or privileges, and that, in the absence of other classes of stock having superior rights, represents the complete interest in the corporation. *Preferred stock* has different characteristics from, and is entitled to certain preferences over, common stock. Preferred stock is entitled to a priority over other stock in the distribution of profits, being entitled to dividends of a definite percentage or amount.

The usual practice for a small corporation is to issue only common stock. It is also recommended that you authorize the issuance of the maximum number of shares for the minimum filing fee. It is wise to issue only a limited number of shares to stockholders in the beginning and save some stock in the treasury.

All corporations must act and contract by means of its officers, agents, and employees. They either can hold corporate offices or be agents appointed by the appropriate officials in the regular course of the corporate business. Corporations have the power to appoint agents with full power and authority to do all the things necessary and proper to enter into contracts with other corporations, individuals, or business entities.

THE FOREIGN CORPORATION

We have already discussed the economic and legal hazards, among other disadvantages, of your forming a corporation in a foreign forum — another state or country — to operate business activities in your own state. The additional expenses, which are very substantial in most cases, and the potential exposure to personal as well as corporate liabilities are unnecessary. Moreover, you would be unduly complicating a very simple procedure of incorporating in your own state.

There are many problems you should be aware of in operating as a foreign corporation, whether it is a foreign corporation doing business in your state or your domestic corporation doing business in another state. These include:

- Statutory qualification procedures and requirements along with the attendant expenses
- Civil and criminal penalties for failure to comply
- Potential fines and personal liabilities
- Exposure to service of process in another state
- Potential taxation hazards
- Payment of resident agent fees, and others

AFTER YOU FORM YOUR CORPORATION

As a corporate officer, director, agent, or employee, you are not personally liable or responsible for corporate debts, obligations, and liabilities because a corporation is a separate business entity from the incorporators, shareholders, and corporate officials. This is one of the magic qualities about a corporation that makes it so popular as a business organization in this country. The general principle of law is unquestioned.

As a corporate official, however, you should know about those areas of the law involving corporate activities that might make you personally liable for corporate debts and that, indeed, can subject you and your corporation to civil and criminal fines and penalties.

Did you know that, in some cases, you can be personally liable, as a matter of law, on "hot checks" issued by your corporation? You can be held personally liable on a great variety of liabilities and obligations of your corporation in some situations. Corporate officials may be held personally liable or responsible in the following situations, among others:

- Failure to register to do business in a foreign state where the corporation does business
- Failure to pay state franchise taxes and file reports with the state
- Failure to keep proper corporate minutes, books, and records
- Failure to issue stock
- Failure to provide adequate capital for the corporate activities
- Failure to sign a corporate check or note properly
- Failure to pay employee withholding taxes to the IRS

PIERCING THE CORPORATE VEIL

The general rule of law, with few exceptions, is that corporate entity, with attendant corporate attributes, will be recognized and not disregarded. There is, however, an exception to the rule. A corporate entity will not be recognized if it produces unjust or undesirable consequences inconsistent with the purpose of the separate entity concept.

The term *piercing the corporate veil* and many other expressions indicate that the web of the corporate entity may be brushed aside by the courts. Some of the other name tags used by the courts include:

- Breaking up the corporate shell
- Penetrating the corporate shield
- Disregarding the corporate entity
- Alter ego
- Formality
- Fraud on the law
- Nominal identity
- Subterfuge

You might wonder why I stress the importance of forming your corporation correctly if a court can come along and tear it all apart. There are some good answers, which you need to know in order to avoid the problem.

The legal rule of law of piercing the corporate veil might sound inconsistent and puzzling, but it is vital that you understand it. This quagmire — this complex and precarious rule of law, all the double-talk, the high-sounding phrases, and the apparent inconsistency — is really a result of the courts being faced with a very tough legal problem: how to create, by a legal fiction, the separate entity of a corporation, and at the same time prevent people from using the device to do wrong.

The legal doctrine that a court may disregard the corporate entity in specified cases is a common-law rule developed by the judges; there are no statutes that directly control the application of the rule. Essentially, most cases are "fact-finding" contests, that is, the court or jury makes a finding of fact in each case based upon the evidence presented. Although each case must rest on its special facts, the courts have developed broad general categories of cases — with infinite variations — as general rules, guides, or guidelines for the application of the doctrine. There are six general categories of cases in which the courts will disregard the corporate entity. They are:

- Where the fiction is used to promote a fraud
- Where the corporate fiction is resorted to as a means of evading an existing legal obligation
- Where the corporate fiction is employed to achieve or promote a monopoly
- Where the corporate fiction is used to circumvent a statute
- Where the corporate fiction is relied upon as a protection of crime or to justify wrong
- Where a corporation is organized and operated as a mere tool or business conduit of another corporation

Insofar as you are personally concerned, there are certain telling signs that courts look for in assisting them to determine the status of any particular case. They are:

- Where the stockholders ignore the formalities of a running corporation (for example, failure to hold meetings, failure to record minutes, etc.)
- Where the stockholders ignore the existence of the corporation, for example, by mixing personal and corporate funds, by dealing with the corporation's customers as if

they were the stockholders' customers, or treating the corporate debts and income as their own.

- Where the corporation is inadequately financed, for example, where the stockholders do not contribute enough capital so that there is a reasonable likelihood that the corporation cannot pay its debts.

The mechanical application of some legal formula in determining the invalidity of a corporation is inherently dangerous. As a practical matter, because of the ingenuity and imagination of American business owners, there is no general formula to fit all cases. One court made this observation about the application of the rule:

> The general rules of law with respect to the piercing of the corporate veil and disregarding the corporate entity are well established, but they offer very little aid when it comes to the decision of a particular case. The decisions are framed in broad principles and there are various theories used to justify the piercing.[3]

If you form your own corporation in accordance with your state's statutes, have adequate capitalization, keep proper corporate records, and avoid the fraud and wrongdoing that might cause the piercing of the corporate veil, you should have no difficulties in operating in the corporate world of limited personal liability.

---

[3]National Bond Finance Co. v. General Motors Corp., 238 F.W. 248, affirmed 341 F 2d 1022.

FORM 9: ARTICLES OF INCORPORATION

We, the undersigned, natural persons of the age of _____ years or more, acting as incorporators of a corporation under the laws of the state of _____, adopt the following articles of incorporation for such corporation:

First: The name of the corporation is _____*(Name)*_____ .

Second: The period of its duration is _____ .

Third: The purpose or purposes for which the corporation is organized are _____ .

Fourth: The aggregate number of shares which the corporation shall have authority to issue is _____*(Amount)*_____ .

Fifth: The corporation will not commence business until at least _____ Dollars have been received by it as consideration for the issuance of shares.

Sixth: Cumulative voting of shares of stock [is], [is not] authorized.

Seventh: Provisions limiting or denying to shareholders the preemptive right to acquire additional or treasury shares of the corporation are: _____
_____ .

Eighth: Provisions for the regulation of the internal affairs of the corporation are: _____ .

Ninth: The address of the initial registered office of the corporation is _____*(Address)*_____ , and the name of its initial registered agent at such address is
_____*(Name)*_____ .

Tenth: Address of the principal place of business is *(Address)*
_____ .

Eleventh: The number of directors constituting the initial board of directors of the corporation is _____, and the names and addresses of the persons who are to serve as directors until the first annual meeting of shareholders or until their successors are elected and shall qualify are:

Name	Address
_____	_____
_____	_____
_____	_____

Twelfth: The name and address of each incorporator is:

Name	Address
_____	_____
_____	_____
(Date) _____	_____
	_____
	_____
	Incorporators

(Verification) _____

FORM 10: WAIVER OF NOTICE
OF THE ORGANIZATION MEETING

We, the undersigned, being all the incorporators [and/or the members of the board of directors] named in the Articles of Incorporation of the above corporation [and/or the stockholders], hereby agree and consent that the organization meeting thereof be held on the date and the time and place stated below and hereby waive all notice of such meeting and of any adjournment thereof.

Place of Meeting: _____

Date of Meeting: _____

Time of Meeting: _____

(Date) _____   _____
                            (Signature)
                          _____
                            (Signature)
                          _____
                            (Signature)

FORM 11: MINUTES OF THE ORGANIZATION MEETING

The organization meeting of the incorporators [and/or the stockholders and/or the members of the board of directors] of _____*(Name)*_____ was held at

_____*(Address)*_____ on

_____*(Date)*_____ at _____*(Time)*_____

The following were present: _____*(Name)*_____

_____*(Name)*_____

_____*(Name)*_____

being all the incorporators [and/or the stockholders and/or the members of the board of directors] of the corporation.

_____*(Name)*_____ was appointed chairman of the meeting and _____*(Name)*_____ was appointed secretary.

The secretary then presented and read to the meeting the waiver of notice of the meeting, subscribed by all the persons named in the Articles of Incorporation, and it was ordered that it be appended to the minutes of the meeting.

The secretary then presented and read to the meeting a copy of the Articles of Incorporation and reported that on

_____*(Date)*_____ the original thereof was filed in the office of the Secretary of State of this state. The copy of the Articles of Incorporation was ordered appended to the minutes of the meeting.

The chairman then stated that nominations were in order for election of directors of the corporation to hold office until the first annual meeting of stockholders and until their successors shall be elected and shall qualify.

The following persons were nominated: _____*(Name)*_____

_____*(Name)*_____

_____*(Name)*_____

No further nominations being made, nominations were closed and a vote was taken. After the vote had been counted, the chairman declared that the foregoing named nominees were elected directors of the corporation.

The secretary then presented to the meeting a proposed form of bylaws which were read to the meeting, considered, and upon motion duly made, seconded and carried, were adopted as and for the bylaws of the corporation and ordered appended to the minutes of the meeting.

Upon motion duly made, seconded, and unanimously carried, it was

Further Resolved, that the specimen stock certificate presented to the meeting be and hereby is adopted as the form of certificate of stock to be issued to represent shares in the corporation:

Further Resolved, that the corporate record book, including the stock transfer ledger, be and hereby is adopted as the record book, stock transfer book, and ledger of the corporation;

Further resolved, that the board of directors be and hereby is authorized to issue the unsubscribed capital stock of the corporation at such time and in such amounts as it shall determine, and to accept the payment thereof, in cash or services or such other property as the board may deem necessary for the business of the corporation;

Further Resolved, that the corporate seal presented to the meeting by the secretary be and the same is hereby adopted as the seal of the corporation;

Further Resolved, that the corporation be and hereby is authorized and directed to accept the payment of capital required for the commencement of business, and that the same be properly reflected upon the books and records of the corporation;

Further Resolved, that the principal office of the corporation be and hereby is designated as
_____*(Address)*_____ and the board of directors is hereby authorized to change said designation as it deems proper and it may designate branch offices from time to time as it shall, in its judgment, determine to be necessary and proper;

Further Resolved, that a plan for the issuance of common stock of the corporation to qualify under the provisions of Section 1244 of the Internal Revenue Code, which plan was read to the meeting, be and the same is hereby adopted, approved, and confirmed by the corporation, and the officers and directors of the corporation are hereby authorized and directed to take all steps, procedures, and action necessary to implement the plan;

Further Resolved, that all other actions, notifications, publications, filings, and any other procedural requirements for the full authorization of this corporation to commence the business for which it was created be completed by the secretary, and that a record thereof be filed in the corporate records of the corporation.

Upon motion duly made, seconded, and carried, it was

Resolved, that the signing of these minutes shall constitute full ratification thereof and waiver of notice of the meeting by the signatories.

There being no further business before the meeting, on motion duly made, seconded, and carried, the meeting adjourned.

(Date)	*(Signature)*
	Chairman
	(Signature)
	Secretary

FORM 12: CALL AND WAIVER
OF NOTICE OF ORGANIZATIONAL MEETING

We, the undersigned, being all of the directors [and/or the incorporators and/or the stockholders] of
_____ *(Name)* _____ , hereby call the organizational meeting of the corporation, to consider and transact any business whatsoever that may be brought before the meeting, and we hereby fix_____ *(Address)* _____ at
_____ *(Time)* _____ as the place of the meeting, and hereby waive any and all requirements by statute, bylaws, or otherwise, as to notice of the time, place, and purposes of the meeting, and consent that the meeting be held at the time and place set out above and to the transaction thereat or at any adjournment thereof of any business whatsoever that may be brought before the meeting, including, without any limitation on the scope of the foregoing, the adoption of bylaws, election of officers, and authorization of issuance of stock.

_____ *(Date)* _____   _____ *(Signature)* _____

FORM 13: NOTICE OF REGULAR MEETING
OF THE BOARD OF DIRECTORS

Notice is hereby given that the regular [annual] meeting of the board of directors of _____ *(Name)* _____ is hereby called to be held at _____ *(Place)* _____ on
_____ *(Date)* _____ at _____ *(Time)* _____ ,
which meeting shall be for the purpose of _____.

_____ *(Date)* _____   _____ *(Signature)* _____
                                              Secretary

FORM 14: RESIGNATION OF OFFICERS AND DIRECTORS

We, the undersigned, hereby tender our resignations as officers and directors of _____ *(Name)* _____ to take effect immediately.

_____ *(Date)* _____   _____ *(Signatures)* _____

Chapter 18

How To Prepare Your Own Partnership Agreement

It is very easy and inexpensive to establish a partnership. In fact, it can be done with nothing more than a handshake and a vague, general understanding that the partners will work together in a business venture with the hope and expectation of making money. The ease of entering into a partnership should not mislead you, however. There can be unexpected consequences. Serious legal responsibilities and liabilities are involved in becoming a partner in any business organization. The fact that you might have full and complete trust and confidence in your partner does not safeguard you from the legal liabilities that you will assume as a partner.

No matter how well you know your prospective partners, no matter how honest they are, it is essential that you prepare your partnership agreement so as to avoid any future misunderstandings and the legal entanglements that too often follow.

A partnership is not only a legal relationship, it is also a personal relationship or status. Before entering upon a partner relationship, the people involved should consider the advantages and disadvantages of this type of business organization, as compared with those of the corporation.

Benjamin Franklin once said:

Partnerships often finish in quarrels; but I was happy in this, that mine were all carried on and ended amicably, owing I think, a good deal to the precaution of having very explicitly settled in our articles everything to be done by, or expected from each partner, so there was nothing to dispute, which precaution I would therefore recommend to all who enter into partnerships.

The Uniform Partnership Act defines *partnership* as "an association of two or more persons to carry on as co-owners a business for profit." Another definition is:

A partnership is a contract of two or more competent persons to place their money, effects, labor, and skill in lawful commerce or business, and to divide the profit and bear the loss in certain proportions; it is a contractual relationship between individuals in which the members ordinarily possess the power to do, in business, what individuals can and usually do in such business, except as specifically limited by the partnership contract or denied by law.

To state that partners are co-owners of a business means each has the power of ultimate control. To determine if a particular association is a partnership, the test is whether the parties, acting in good faith and with a business purpose, intend to join together to conduct the enterprise. All the facts must be considered: the agreement, the conduct of the parties in carrying out its provisions, their statements, the testimony of disinterested persons, the relationship of the parties, their respective abilities and capital contributions, the sharing of profits and losses, the actual control of the business, and any other facts highlighting the true intent of the parties. When employed, this test presents a difficult problem, particularly if the parties want to share the profits, but not the losses, or if they want to share the income, but not the control.

Frequently, people want the benefits of a partnership, but not the liabilities. During the development of the laws of partnership in England from 1600 to 1850, it was held that the receipt by a person of a share of the profits of the business was enough to make him a partner, but this objective test, easy to apply, was soon rejected as unworkable. Sharing profits is, indeed, a very important factor. For example, according to the Uniform Partnership Act, it is *prima facie* evidence that the person receiving a share of the profits is a partner in the business, except where the profits are received as payment for a debt, wages, rent, annuity to a widow or representative of a deceased partner, interest on a loan, consideration for the sale of good will.

TYPES OF PARTNERSHIPS

A *limited partnership* is one in which the liability of some members, but not all, is limited. Such a partnership may be formed under most state statutes that permit an individual to contribute a specific sum of money to the capital of the partnership and limit his liability for losses to that amount. The partnership must otherwise comply with the requirements of the statute.

For tax purposes, the term *partnership* includes a syndicate, group, pool, joint venture, or other unincorporated organization through or by means of which any business, financial operation, or venture is carried on, and that is not a corporation or a trust or estate. This definition obviously expands the meaning of the term under the definitions given previously, but only for tax purposes.

A partnership as an entity is not subject to an income tax. It must file an annual return stating specifically the items of its gross income and allowable deductions, but this return is for informational purposes only and no payment is required. The taxable income of a partnership is computed in the same manner as in the case of an individual, except that income and loss must be itemized according to derivation and certain deductions are not allowed.

The individual partners are liable for the payment of income tax. Each partner reports the tax due on his share of partnership income on his own individual return. A partner's share of partnership income is generally determined by the partnership agreement.

A *family partnership* is one whose members are closely related by blood or marriage. Family partnerships are sometimes created to shift income from the organizer of a business to members of his family. Shifting income reduces the family taxes if the family members are in lower tax brackets. Although tax saving is sometimes the primary motive for the partnership, the Internal Revenue Service will recognize the arrangement if the family members actually own their partnership interests. This depends on the intent of the parties, determined from all the facts: the agreement; the relationship of the parties; their conduct, statements, individual abilities, and capital contributions; who controls the income and how it is used; and any other facts showing their true intent of the partners.

A family partnership is frequently used where capital is material income-producing factor, for example, a firm that requires large inventories or investments in plant and equipment. The Internal Revenue Service will recognize the family member if he actually owns a capital interest, even if he got it from another family member, provided the transaction vested him with dominion and control.

The donor may retain substantial powers as managing partner if other facts show that he really gave up part of his interest and made the donee its true owner. In the family partnership where the business income is primarily from fees, commissions, or other pay for personal services, the IRS generally will not recognize the family member unless he contributes substantial or necessary services.

CONSIDERATIONS

In your consideration of a partnership as a business entity, you should keep in mind that you are exposed to personal liability in all business transactions. Therefore, you should be very careful in the selection of your partners, and be sure you have adequate insurance coverage. In tax matters, the question of whether a partnership exists will depend on the definitions set out in the Internal Revenue Code.

When the courts are presented with the question of whether a partnership exists in specific fact situations, they generally look for the following four essentials:

- Two or more parties intending to be partners
- Sharing of profits and losses
- Joint ownership and control of capital assets or property of the group
- Joint control and management of the business

The duties and obligations of partners arising from a partnership agreement are regulated as far as they are covered by the written contract. A written agreement between partners constitutes the measure of each partner's rights and obligations. The written agreement may include practically any provision you desire as long as it is lawful. Where the written agreement does not cover situations or questions that arise, they are determined under applicable statutory law. If a question is not answered by the provisions of the statutes, it will be controlled by common-law rules.

You can benefit from all of the past disputes and mistakes between partners if you study the rules and understand and appreciate the problems that might arise. It is very easy to prepare a partnership agreement. Most written agreements begin with the date, the identification of the parties, a statement of the place of residence of each, and a statement of the purpose and intention of the written document. ALthough this information is not absolutely essential to the validity of a contract, it is important and helpful, and should appear at some place in the document. There are many different forms and provisions you can use. The one I recommend is provided at the end of this chapter.

DISSOLUTION OF A PARTNERSHIP

Although courts and lawyers are not always precise in distinguishing among the various terms that apply to the process leading to the final settlement of all partnership affairs, the authors of the Uniform Act suggest the following delineation: *Dissolution* designates that point in time when the partners cease to carry on the business together. *Winding up,* often called liquidation, is the process of settling partnership affairs after dissolution. *Termination* is the point at which all the partnership affairs are wound up.

The Uniform Act defines *dissolution* as the change in the relation of the partners caused by any partner ceasing to be associated in the carrying on of the business. Dissolution is not in itself a termination of the partnership or of the rights and powers of partners, for many of these persist during the winding up process. Rather, the term describes the change in the partnership relation that ultimately results in its termination.

The dissolution of a partnership can be caused or required by any number of things, including the following:

- The operation of law
- Termination of term or purpose

- The will of one partner
- Mutual consent
- The admission of a new partner
- The withdrawal or retirement of a partner
- The expulsion or exclusion of a partner
- The assignment of a partner's interest in the partnership
- The assignment of a partner's property rights
- The sale or transfer of firm effects
- Changes in the personal status of partners
- Bankruptcy or insolvency

Winding up means the administration of assets for the purpose of terminating the business and discharging the obligations of the partnership to its members. However, although the provisions of the Uniform Act relating to the application of partnership property on dissolution are concerned with a discontinuance of the day-to-day business, they do not forbid other methods of winding up a partnership. For example, a provision for withdrawal of a partner might be considered a type of winding up of a partnership without the necessity of discounting the daily business.

Where a partnership is ended by mutual consent or by the expiration of its term, the right to wind up is vested in all the partners. In that case, each partner is under a duty to liquidate partnership affairs, which would include the performance of existing contracts, the collection of debts or claims due the firm, and the payment of the firm's debts.

One of the ordinary duties of partners is to keep true and correct books showing the firm's accounts, such books being at all times open to the inspection of all the members of the firm. According to the Uniform Act, the partnership book must be kept, subject to any agreement between the partners, at the principal place of business of the partnership, and every partner at all times must have access to and may inspect and copy any of them. This provision refers to an active partnership. When a partnership is dissolved, the firm's books and records belong to all of the partners.

In settling accounts between partners after dissolution, the Uniform Act states that the liabilities of the partnership rank in payment as follows:

- Those owed to creditors other than partners

- Those owed to partners other than for capital and profits
- Those owed to partners in respect of capital
- Those owed to partners in respect of profits

The statutory rules for distribution of assets are applicable only in the absence of an agreement between the partners specifying some other method of distribution.

FORM 15: PARTNERSHIP AGREEMENT

(Introductory Clause) This agreement of partnership is made and entered into this _____ day of _____, 19____, by and between _____ *(Name)* _____, _____ *(Name)* _____, _____ *(Name)* _____, and _____ *(Name)* _____ of the City of _____, County of _____, State of _____, who witness and agree as follows:

1. (Name of Partnership or Business) The firm name of the said partnership shall be _____ *(Name)* _____ .

2. (Duration) This partnership shall continue for the term of _____ years from the date of this agreement.

3. (Place of Business) The partnership business and operations shall be carried on at _____ *(Address)* _____ , or such other place as the partnership shall from time to time determine.

4. (Purpose) This partnership shall be for the purpose of buying, selling, and dealing in _____.

5. (Capital) The capital of the partnership shall be _____ Dollars, and each partner shall contribute equally thereto (or in such shares as may from time to time be agreed upon in writing).

6. (Advances) Any partner may from time to time, with the consent of the others, advance any sums of money to the firm by way of loan, and every such advance shall bear interest at the rate of _____ percent per annum, from the time of making the advance until repayment thereof, and may be withdrawn at any time on _____ months' notice.

7. (Expenses) All rent, expenses for repairs or improvements, taxes, premiums of insurance, salaries and wages, and any and all other reasonable and necessary expenses, losses, and damages which may be incurred in carrying on the partnership business (and the interest on the capital, payable to the respective partners), shall be paid out of the receipts and earnings of the said business, and in case such receipts and earnings are insufficient to pay such charges, the said partners shall contribute thereto in the shares or proportions in which they are entitled to the profits of the business.

8. (Profits, Compensation, and Drawing Accounts) Each partner herein shall share in all profits or losses of the business in the same proportions as his share in the capital of the firm bears to the total capital of the firm.

9. (Regular Meetings) On _____ *(Day)* _____ of each week, at _____ *(Time)* _____ , there shall be a meeting of the partners, at the office of the firm, for the purpose of going over expense accounts for the preceding week, and for the further purpose of discussing and acting upon the general conduct of the business of the partnership. For any matters within the scope of the business, and within this or supplemental contracts, a majority of the partners present at any such meeting shall prevail. Any change of the scope or nature of the business, however, shall not be made except by and with the knowledge and consent of all of the partners.

10. (Books and Accounts) Proper books of accounts shall be kept at the office of the firm, in which shall be entered all the dealings and transactions of the partnership. The books shall at all times be open to the inspection of all or any of the partners, and be kept constantly posted and current.

11. (Restrictions on Authority of Partners) No partner, without the previous consent in writing of the others, shall buy or sell or enter into any contract for the purchase or sale of any goods or other articles amounting to the value of _____ Dollars or more.

12. (Retirement of Partner) Any partner may retire at any time from the partnership, upon giving written notice of his intention to do so, to the other partners personally, and the partnership shall determine as to him _____ months after the date of said notice; but the other partners may purchase his interest at a fair valuation and carry on the business.

13. (Dissolution) In case the net assets of the partnership shall at any time fall below the sum of _____ Dollars, then any member thereof, in spite of the fact that the partnership has not expired by lapse of time, may withdraw from the firm, and commence an action for the dissolution of the firm.

(Close of Contract) In Witness Whereof, we hereunto set our hands, this _____ day of _____, 19_____, at
_____.

(Signature)	*(Signature)*
Partner	Partner
(Signature)	*(Signature)*
Partner	Partner

Chapter 19

Negotiating
and Preparing Contracts

We all enter into many contracts each day without giving it much thought. Whether you buy a house, sell a car, pick up a loaf of bread at the corner store, or go out to dinner, you do it all in accordance with implied or written legal contracts. When you catch a cab, pay your telephone bill, hop an airplane to Las Vegas, you do it in accordance with a legal contract.

Lawyers, judges, professors, law students, and writers spend a great deal of time talking, debating, arguing, and discussing the definition of a contract. It is easy to give a legal textbook definition, but the problem most of us have is determining whether a transaction comes within that definition. The professors define a *contract* as a promise, or set of promises, for breach of which the law gives a remedy, or for the performance of which the law in some way recognizes a duty. This is a little like saying a contract is a valid agreement. The professors usually proceed to elaborately explain the essential elements of a contract, which are:

- A valid offer
- An acceptance of the offer
- Valid consideration
- Legal capacity of the respective parties
- Legal subject matter
- A writing, if required by law

This description of a contract might not be as elusive as the "I know one when I see it" definition, but you should understand that the big problem results from the difficulty that most people have in agreeing on the adequacy or sufficiency of these essential elements of a contract.

Typically, a controversy can develop where two contracting parties agree that there must be consideration to have a legal contract, but they disagree as to what constitutes consideration in a given case. Was there an offer? Was there an acceptance? Was the consideration adequate? It is important for you, in negotiating and preparing your contracts, to be familiar with the general principles of law governing these elements.

OFFER AND ACCEPTANCE

An *offer* is the communication of one person, the *offeror*, to another person, the *offeree,* of an intent to enter into a mutual agreement based upon definite and certain terms. An offer may be revoked or withdrawn before acceptance by the offeree. An *acceptance* is simply a communication by the offeree to the offeror that the offer is accepted. The acceptance must be absolute and must be strictly in accord with the terms of the offer.

If other conditions or terms are included in an attempted acceptance, it constitutes a *counteroffer* for another contract. This is one of the "hot" items for litigation because many people, after a long series of discussions and negotiations, tend to remember only those discussions involving their own ideas and thoughts. Put in more pragmatic terms, two people do not remember the same things from the same discussion.

In addition to the usual offer and acceptance, which form a bilateral contract, there is the *unilateral contract*. This is an offer in which the offeror does not receive a return promise as consideration for the contract. Instead, he receives something other than a promise or assent, such as an act or performance.

CONSIDERATION

A dictionary definition of *consideration* is "the inducement to a contract, or other legal transaction; an act or forbearance or the promise thereof done or give by one party in return for the act or promise of another."[1]

Many people think of consideration as a payment of money or other thing of value. A more legal definition is that consideration is a legal benefit to the promisor or a legal detriment to the promisee. It might be a forbearance; a creation, modification, or distruction of a legal relationship; or a return promise.

LEGAL CAPACITY OF PARTIES

As a general rule, any adult person has the legal capacity to enter into a valid contract. Incompetency, minority (usually defined as under the age of 18), fraud and duress, or other such matters usually bring into question the capacity of parties to enter into contracts. The general description of persons in the community as a "crazy" does not necessarily make them incompetent to enter into contracts. If a person understands the full nature of the transaction into which he is entering, the courts generally find legal capacity to contract.

LEGAL SUBJECT MATTER

A contract, to be enforceable by the courts, must involve legal subject matter or transactions. If an agreement relates to the doing of an illegal or unlawful act, such as gambling (in most states) or violation of statutes, public policy, or other laws, it is not legal, valid, or enforceable. This is an often overlooked factor in preparing contracts. You should be alert to any transaction that might be contrary to zoning laws, permit requirements, consumer protection acts, the uniform commercial code, usury statutes, or other applicable laws and regulations.

STATUTE OF FRAUDS

As a general rule, verbal agreements are valid, legal, and enforceable. Even so, you probably know the importance of writing all contracts and having them signed by the parties. You should develop this habit in your business transactions. It simplifies the resolution of many disputes and differences that can occur.

---

[1]*Webster's Ninth New Collegiate Dictionary,* 1985

The Statutes of Frauds, enacted in all 50 states, is based upon the English statutes enacted in 1677, called "An Act for the Prevention of Frauds and Perjuries." Although most of the provisions of the statutes have been repealed in England, except those for land and guaranty contracts, in the United States, a wide variety of these have been statutes. The usual subjects covered include provisions that some contracts, in order to be valid, must be in writing. These contracts include:

- Contracts for interest in land
- Contracts that by the terms are not to be performed within 1 year after the making of the contract
- Contracts constituting a promise to answer for the debt, default, or miscarriage of another

GOVERNMENTAL CONTROL OF SUBJECT MATTER

Contracts are as easy to make as they are to break. Almost any manifestation of intent by the parties — verbal or written — will result in a valid contract as long as it has the elements that make up a contract.

A contract might be invalid or unenforceable because it violates public policy or some provision of a federal or state statute or ordinance, such as a prohibition against gambling, excessive interest, consumer acts, or regulatory rulings. The basic principle of law and its significance on this point are extremely important for all contracts. The rule was stated by the United States Supreme Court as follows:

It is . . . settled that the laws which subsist at the time and place of the making of a contract, and where it is to be performed, enter into and form a part of it as if they were expressly referred to and incorporated in its terms. This principle embraces alike those which affect its validity, construction, discharge, and enforcement.[2]

In another context, the same court said:

Contracts, however expressed, cannot fetter the constitutional authority of the Congress. Contracts may create rights

---

[2]Von Hoffman v. City of Quincy, 4 Wall. 535, 71 U.S. 535

of property, but when contracts deal with a subject matter which lies within the control of the Congress, they have a congenital infirmity. Parties cannot remove their transactions from the reach of dominant constitutional power by making contracts about them.[3]

Another court said it this way:

> . . . all contracts are entered into subject to the proper exercise of a reserved police power of the state.[4]

The rule of *reserved police power* or *congenital infirmity* of contracts applies with equal force to federal and state constitutions, statutes, and regulations, as well as local governing rules, regulations, and ordinances. There is a constitutional provision which provides that no state shall pass any law "impairing the obligation of contracts." There have been many sophisticated and esoteric legal arguments about the apparent conflict between the two constitutional provisions, but presently the *police power of the State* clearly carries the day.

Any contract that contains an element which is illegal or prohibited either by virtue of statute, the Constitution, or an ordinance—or as against public policy—presents serious legal problems for both parties. For example, suppose an owner of land entered into a contract with a contractor for the construction of a house. If the contractor does not have a proper license or cannot get a permit to build the house or the zoning laws prohibit houses on the lot selected, there can be legal problems or lawsuits later. Suppose you enter into a contract with a person who is 17 years of age in a state where the legal age of majority is 18. You lose!

Suppose, further, that you entered into a contract with a "common carrier" trucking line regulated by the Interstate Commerce Commission to ship a truckload of goods from Phoenix, Arizona, to New York City for $1,000. If the regulatory tariff prescribes a rate of $3,000 for that item, the truck line can sue you and collect $3,000. That is the law! Your contract is subject to the control of the government regulations. The reserved police power of the state will prevail.

---

[3] Norman v. Baltimore and Ohio Railroad Company, 294 U.S. 240, 30708
[4] 164 Colo. 424, 435 P 2d 412, 416 (1967)

186

It is essential that you avoid these entanglements by checking all available information before you enter into a contract. It is important to know the subject matter of a contract, and it is equally important to know the person with whom you are dealing.

CHANGES IN CONTRACTS

The parties to a contract may modify it or waive their rights under it and agree to terms under a new or modified contract. The changes must be supported by consideration, as in any contract. It is always wise to have changes made in writing.

LEGAL INTERPRETATION AND MEANING OF TERMS

In determining what a paragraph, a sentence, a phrase, or a word in a contract means, the courts generally will apply the following principles: Effect must be given to the intention of the parties as gathered from the construction of the entire contract. The contract should receive a practical interpretation by the courts. Where a contract is understood by one of the parties in a certain sense and the other party knows that he so understands it, then that is how the undertaking will be interpreted, provided this can be done without making a new contract. The parties may, in writing the contract itself, define the terms used.

Written matter in a contract controls printed matter where the two are inconsistent, but the courts will consider both if possible. A statute, regulation, tariff, or ordinance prescribing subject matter regulations is considered a part of the contract. If the terms of the contract are clear and unambiguous, the court is bound to enforce the contract. Clauses in contracts providing for penalties or excessive liquidated damages for default or nonperformance are not favored by the courts, and are strictly construed. Therefore, it is suggested that you not rely too heavily on these provisions.

BREACH OF CONTRACT

If you enter into a contract and something does go wrong, you should know your rights and be prepared to handle the problem without further losses, confusion, and bewilderment. If you have a good contract, the "lawsuit" or dispute generally can be resolved without extensive litigation and acrimony. Typically, the most common breach of contract consists of failure to pay money in accordance with the contract, and failure or refusal to perform in accordance with the contract. Some of the typical disputes that lead to these breaches of contract include:

- One party wanting more money
- One party wanting more work, services, or goods
- Partial or complete repudiation of the contract by one party
- Disagreements over quality of goods, work, or materials
- The so-called "excuses" for nonperformance

The typical problem that results in a nasty lawsuit usually can be avoided if the parties know their own business and benefit from the past. They should make provisions in the contract for the resolution of as many contingencies as they can reasonably anticipate.

RECOVERABLE DAMAGES

What happens when one party breaches a contract? If it does not cause the other party some damage or injury, not much will happen. Many people fail to live up to the promises they make, but this does not always result in a lawsuit. There are several reasons:

- Lawsuits are very expensive for everybody
- Lawsuits are unpleasant for both sides
- Lawsuits take a lot of time
- Lawsuits can range from embarrassing to downright stultifying
- Letting a jury decide a business dispute is like flipping a coin
- Assessment of damages is difficult for any judge, any jury and both parties

The rule of law on what one party is entitled to recover from another who breaches a contract is easier to state than it is to apply to actual cases — just like the difficulty in deciding if there is a contract. In 1854, the famous English case of *Hadley v. Baxendale* gave a classic statement of the rule that is followed today by most courts in this country. The court announced:

Where two parties have made a contract which one of them has broken, the damages which the other party ought to receive in respect of such breach of contract should be such as may fairly and reasonably be considered either arising naturally, i.e., according to the usual course of things, from such breach of contract itself, or such as may reasonably be supposed to have been in the contemplation of both parties, at the time they made the contract, as the probable result of the breach of it.[5]

Today, the typical jury instruction given by trial judges in these cases is to award "compensation for whatever loss or injury directly and proximately results from the defendant's wrongful act." The imagination of your lawyer in presenting the evidence, as well as the quality of your evidence on the damage issue, will be a major factor in the outcome of your lawsuit. Thus, your main problem in a lawsuit involving breach of contract is to produce evidence of all the damages you sustain and convince the jury you are entitled to compensation for all of them. This is a tough job. It is better to spend extra time in negotiating and preparing a good contract in your favor.

DISCHARGE OR RESCISSION OF CONTRACTS

Contracts can be discharged in many ways, including:

- Performance
- Breach
- Impossibility of performance
- Novation or change of agreement
- Operation of law
- Recission based on fraud, mistake, duress, or undue influence

Contracts may be rescinded by agreement of the parties or pursuant to statutes. An innocent party may rescind at his election, upon a number of grounds, including default, excessive delays, repudiation, inability to perform, willful refusal to perform, fraud, misrepresentation, or mutual mistake.

The right of a party to rescind a contract should be exer-

---

[5]Hadley v. Baxendale, 9 EX 341, 156 Eng Rep 145, 151 (1854)

cised promptly upon discovery of the pertinent facts. If the right is not exercised within a reasonable time, it might be waived. The effect of rescission is to end the contract. It is annihilated so effectively that, in the eyes of the law, it never had an existence.

HOW TO PREPARE CONTRACTS

As we have seen, the essential elements of a valid contract consist of:

- Mutual assent
- Consideration
- Competent parties having legal capacity to contract in relation to the subject matter involved in the transaction
- Absence of any statute or rule of the common law that declares the particular transaction to be void or illegal

As a practical matter, the actual preparation of a contract involves a lot more than the legal essentials. The actual parts of a contract are:

- The name of the document
- Introductory remarks — names of the parties, the date, and recitations that it is an agreement
- Recitals — statements of facts upon which the contract is based, representation of the parties, or setting the stage; the "Whereas Clause," as it is called
- The operative provisions — the specific items agreed upon by the parties: this is the most important part
- Closing — signatures and dates; some prefer to date both at the top and the bottom of the contract, but one date is enough
- Witnesses, if any, but not required in most contracts
- Acknowledgments, if any, but not required in some contracts.

ITEMS TO CONSIDER
IN NEGOTIATING AND PREPARING CONTRACTS

- Negotiate all the provisions you want before you sign a contract. If possible, have the contract state the legal remedies if the other party defaults.

- Give each contract a name for identification, even though the promises in the contract, not the name, govern the obligations and rights of the parties.
  Obtain fact recitals from the other party. Make sure you know each fact to be true before you agree to it.
- Carefully identify each party. Make sure you know with whom you are dealing. If you are contracting with an individual, do you want, or need, the signature of his spouse? If so, try to name the spouse as a party to the contract.
- Get the names of each partner in a partnership. If possible, have each general partner sign, or at least the managing partner.
- Carefully identify any corporation with which you are making a contract. The contract should show the exact corporate name and, if possible, the state of incorporation. Make sure you can read the signatures of the officers or agents. Consider the need for a corporate resolution authorizing the corporation to sign.
- If you are dealing with a trustee, incompetent, receiver, or executor, make sure the agreement reflects the entity that is assuming the obligations of the contract.
- Where there are two parties on the other side, you usually will want to make them jointly and severally liable.
- If you are one of two or more parties on the same side of a contract, you usually will want a separate contract with your coparty to define your rights and duties.
- If you are an agent, be sure you sign as agent.
- Make sure you can read all signatures.
- Obtain and keep a fully signed and completed contract. Your copy should be identical with the copy the other side has. It is wise to keep a copy of a document, such as a deed, even if the other side has the only signed document, or even if it is recorded. Your copy should show who, when, and by whom the signed copy was delivered to you and by you to the other party.
- Contracts should be at least long enough to tell you what you should do, when you should do it, and what happens if you do not; what the other party should do, when he should do it, and what happens if he does not.

- It makes no legal difference whether a written contract is printed, typewritten, handwritten, or a combination of these.

The more effort you put into the negotiations and preparation of a good contract, the less time, effort, and money you will need to spend trying to save a bad situation. Investigate and know with whom you are contracting. The most brilliantly negotiated and drafted contract in the world cannot save you if you are dealing with a crook.

Chapter 20

The Development
of Law in America

The term *law,* in its generic sense, means a rule of action or conduct duly prescribed by controlling authority, by the law-making power of the state, by the sovereign power, or by the supreme power of the state. It is that which is laid down, ordained, or established; a rule or method according to which phenomena or actions coexist or follow each other; that which must be obeyed and followed by citizens, subject to sanctions or legal consequences.

An act of the legislature deposited in the office of the secretary of state, properly authenticated by presiding officers of the two houses, and approved by the governor is law. It is a body of principles, standards, and rules promulgated by government.

Law is nothing else than reason; it is the body of rules by which we govern ourselves. The law of a state is found in its statutory and constitutional enactments as interpreted by its courts, and in the absence of statutory law, in the rulings of its courts. The law of the United States is found in its Constitution, the Acts of Congress, and in its treaties — all as interpreted by its courts — and in those matters specially committed to the judicial power of the rulings of its courts.

Justice Oliver Wendell Holmes said:

The rational study of law is . . . to a large extent the study of history.

The life of the law has not been logic; it has been experience. The felt necessities of the time, the prevalent moral and political theories, intuitions of public policy, avowed or unconscious, even the prejudices which judges share with their fellow man have had a good deal more to do than the syllogism in determining the rules by which men should be governed.

Blackstone gave a more formalistic definition of the term *law*. He called it:

A rule of civil conduct prescribed by the supreme power of a state, commanding what is right and prohibiting what is wrong. And, first, it is a rule: not a transient sudden order from a superior to or concerning a particular person; but something permanent, uniform and universal.[1]

Blackstone's definition does not fit our present-day standards, at least to the extent that it makes law depend upon the supreme power of the state. Blackstone's definition is not compatible with the genius of our form of government; neither is it literally true as applicable to our system. In our system of jurisprudence, we acknowledge no supreme power, except that of the people.

Another interesting (and puzzling) definition of the term law is as follows:

A law may be defined as an assemblage of signs declarative of a volition concerned or adopted by the sovereign in a state, concerning the conduct to be observed in a certain case by a certain person or class of persons, who in the case in question are or are supposed to be subject to his power; such volition trusting for its accomplishment to the expectation of certain events which it is intended such declarative should upon occasion by a means of bringing to pass, and the prospect of which it is intended should act as a motive upon those whose conduct is in question.

The term *natural law* was an expression largely used in the philosophical speculations of the Roman jurists of the Antoine

---

[1]*Blackstone's Commentaries*

Age, and was intended to denote a system of rules and principles for the guidance of human conduct which, independent of enacted law or of the system peculiar to any one people, might be discovered by the rational intelligence of man, and would be found to grow out of and conform to his nature.

It has been said that natural law is a rule that so necessarily agrees with the nature and state of man that, without observing its maxims, the peace and happiness of society can never be preserved.

Law, then, is a set of rules by which a society governs itself.

HISTORICAL BACKGROUND AND DEVELOPMENT OF LAW

Even before men could write, the laws and customs of each community were passed down from one generation to the next by the older members of the group. That was a long time ago, but when you think it through, you can find that the beginning of the history of law is precisely the same date as the dawn of the history of mankind. With some reflection, you will recognize that you cannot name one instance in which any "society" or group of men and women lived any significant period of time without laws or rules. Whether the source of the laws happened to be some chief, a witch doctor, a bloody dictator, the gods of the sky, the Bible, or from some place known as heaven, there is one truth that emerges with the ineluctability of a syllogism: laws are made to encourage us to do what is "good," and avoid that which is "bad." If you want to know how to distinguish between that which is good and that which is bad, just close your eyes, relax, and ask your conscience. You can't miss.

Justice Oliver Wendell Holmes said:

The law is the witness and external deposit of our moral life. Its history is the history of the moral development of the race.

Code of Hammurabi

The earliest law that has been preserved was developed about 2000 B.C. by Hammurabi, a ruler of the ancient Sumerians. The Sumerians lived in the valley of the Tigris and Euphrates rivers. Hammurabi's Code set forth a complete system of law; it set down the kinds of punishment to be used for a variety of offenses; and it established the amounts of payment to be made for various services rendered. If you are a student of history, you will be amazed at how "smart" the people were who inhabited the earth 4,000 years ago.

The Law of Moses

About 1200 B.C., Moses, a Hebrew, hammered out the Ten Commandments, which stated principles of behavior that had long been recognized as good. These Commandments, in one form or another, have had a profound influence on every body of law during all ages of history.

The Law of the Ancient Greeks

The Greeks were among the first to introduce the idea that laws are made by men and therefore can be changed by men whenever the need arises. This idea marked a great step forward in human thought. Before that time, people believed that laws always came from a god or group of gods. They thought that these divine laws were revealed through the rulers or priests and could not be changed by men, even though they might be unjust.

The Greeks respected law more than any other people had done before. They believed that a country should be ruled by law, rather than by men. This basic concept is becoming more elusive for us in our modern society.

Law in Ancient Rome

The Romans made great strides in the development of law. Roman law was more complete, and it was in Rome that the first legal profession developed. The first important step in Roman law came in 450 B.C., when the Law of the Twelve Tables, based on the Roman religion, was prepared by a council of ten men. The laws were inscribed on brass tablets. For hundreds of years many Romans memorized the Twelve Tablets, and the laws were passed from generation to generation.

Modern European Law

The influence of Roman law declined after the fall of the Roman Empire; however, the ideas developed by the Roman and canon law during the Middle Ages still had a profound influence on the laws of most European countries. The Code Napolean also has had a great influence on modern-day laws.

This Code was originally made up of 36 laws brought together under the direction of Napoleon Bonaparte, who in 1803 directed outstanding law writers to collect and simplify into one statement the laws by which France was governed. The Code was completed in 1804, and forms the foundation upon which the whole body of French law is now based. It has had a great influence on the laws of many countries in Western Europe.

American Law

When the English colonists settled in North America, they brought with them the English common law, which formed the basis for American and Canadian law.

Common law is composed of the body of those principles and rules of action relating to the government and security of persons and property which derive their authority solely from usages and customs of immemorial antiquity, or from the judgments and decrees of the courts recognizing, affirming, and enforcing such usages and customs. It is the legal embodiment of practice and common sense whose guiding star is to do what is right.

The nature of the common law requires that each time a rule of law is applied, it be carefully scrutinized to make sure that the conditions and needs of the times have not so changed as to make further application of it the instrument of injustice. Whenever an old rule is found unsuited to present conditions or is unsound, it should be set aside and a rule declared that is in harmony with those conditions and that meets the demands of justice. Justice Cardozo said:

> A rule which in its origin was the creation of the courts themselves, and was supposed in the making to express the mores of the day, may be abrogated by courts when the mores have so changed that perpetuation of the rule would do violence to the social Conscience . . . This is not usurpation. It is not even innovation. It is the reservation for ourselves of the same power of creation that built up the common law through its exercise by the judges of the past.

THE LEGAL SYSTEM IN AMERICA

The English common law has been adopted as the basis of jurisprudence in all the states in the United States except Louisiana, where the civil law (Code of Napoleon) prevails in civil matters. The United States Constitution and the constitutions of the 50 states form the foundations upon which our laws are based.

The United States Constitution establishes the three branches of the federal government—executive, legislative, and judicial—and it establishes the balance of power among those three branches. It sets forth the powers granted to the federal government and the powers reserved for the states. Thus, the Constitution states what cases the federal courts have jurisdiction to handle and leaves all other judicial power to the states.

Whatever may be said, in an historical sense, about the balance of power among the three federal branches of government and the powers reserved to the states, it is plain to most knowledgeable citizens that the federal government has taken unto itself, during the past 45 years, a preponderating and dominant share of all governmental activities relating to every aspect of our lives. There is scarcely any aspect of our daily lives that does not get exposed to the searching light of the intervention of the federal governmental.

Constitutional Law

The basic and fundamental laws of our land are found in the federal and state constitutions. It is far more difficult to change the constitution than it is to enact or change other laws. The United States Constitution can be amended in two ways:

- Two-thirds of the members of both houses of Congress may propose amendments
- On the application of the legislatures of two-thirds of the states, Congress may call a convention for proposing amendments.

Any changes must be ratified by three-fourths of the states or by special conventions in three-fourths of the states.

Each of the state constitutions sets out the basic governmental structure of executive, legislative, and judicial branches. Each of these governmental branches performs certain functions within the guidelines set out in the constitutions.

Statutory Law

The legislatures of each state are the law-making branches of the state, and the United States Congress is the legislative body of the federal government. Each state has a state legislature, as well as county and city governments.

Most of the legislative bodies of the states are divided into two parts, or houses, often called the Senate and House of Representatives, as in the United States Congress, whose members are elected for different terms. Each house must enact a bill before it is sent to the executive to be signed into law or vetoed. The federal and state constitutions provide for the enactment of a bill notwithstanding the veto of the executive branch if a sufficiently large majority of the legislature vote in favor of the bill. This process is known as *overriding a veto*. Laws passed by state legislatures are called *statutes;* those enacted by the local governments usually are called *ordinances*.

Any law passed by the legislative branch may be reviewed by the judicial branch of the government if someone affected by the law asserts that it is contrary to the state or federal constitution. If a court with proper jurisdiction finds that a law is unconstitutional, it becomes inoperative. The power of the courts to examine the constitutionality of laws passed by the legislature is called the *right of judicial review*. It is one of the strongest weapons that citizens have in protecting their constitutional rights. The United States Supreme Court has been very liberal during the past 20 to 40 years in construing the constitution to protect the private rights of the people.

Executive Branch

We usually think of the executive branch of government as that group of workers presided over by our president, the governor, or the mayor. These are the chief executives of that branch of government in the country, state, and city, respectively. The chief executive is usually an elected official who holds office for a term of years specified in the constitution or charter.

It is the responsibility of the executive branch to propose new laws to the legislature, to approve or disapprove laws that have been passed, and to enforce the statutes that are in effect. It is the job of the executive to see that the government operates to protect the interests of the people. Although the executive branch has no power to pass laws, it does set up regulatory and administrative agencies. These agencies are the bodies that proliferate like crabgrass and look over you all the time.

Administrative Law

Administrative law is an area of law that holds a special fascination for me. I have been personally involved in the operation of many of the federal and state agencies. Many of the agencies proceeded on the basis that "more regulation" is good government!

The term *administrative law,* although well recognized by judicial and other authorities and having given rise to an enormous literature and decision-making rulings, has no authoritative definition in English. In one sense, the term embraces everything that the law controls or is intended to control; it is the vast network encompassing the administrative operations of government, including the laws that provide for the structure of government and prescribe its procedure. It embraces the law that governs the methods of legislatures, provides for the existence and operation of the courts and the agencies themselves, governs their procedure, and determines personnel policies in all branches of the government. Administrative law is concerned with the protection of private right, as well as the problems of administrative regulations, rather than those of administrative management.

Administrative law is involved in the legal problems arising out of the existence of agencies, which combine in a single entity the legislative, executive, and judicial powers of government. Even though the civics teachers and the law professors might still claim that the three branches of our federal government are "separate" and "balanced," the administrative agencies perform all three functions with the sweeping power of an emperor.

The primary function of administrative agencies and administrative law is to carry into effect the will of the federal or state government as expressed by its legislature, but one of the most striking facts of administrative agencies generally is the variety of their specific functions. They get involved in every aspect of human activity.

Some of these functions vested in particular administrative agencies embrace those of the legislature, the grand jury, the prosecutor, the policeman, and the courts, and some statutory schemes provide for or permit administrative enforcement. This is what some people refer to as being "prosecutor, judge, and jury." For example, the Federal Trade Commission has been under severe criticism for its alleged arbitrary and unbridled usurpation and misuse of power.

Case Law

Decisions rendered by the various courts are sometimes referred to as *legal precedents;* that is, they become rules of law to apply to the case before the court and to future cases. Judges are, of course, bound by the constitutions, statutes, and laws of the land. There are so many new laws, new cases, and controversies, however, that the judges are grossly overworked in trying to resolve disputes that arise among the citizens.

Many modern judges do not pay too much attention to precedents. Some courts make more new laws than the legislative branches. The Warren court set the stage during the 1950s and 1960s for other courts to ignore legal precedents, and to set out on a course of "liberal" interpretations of the constitutions and statutes to conform to the current popular political ideas of the day. This intrusion of the federal government into the private lives of citizens, along with the expansion of legislative and executive interference into the private rights of people, has brought into question the competency of our government to properly govern.

Chapter 21

How To Do Legal Research

It is not necessary to have any special legal training to do the legal research needed to handle many of the legal problems you encounter. You will need adequate time, interest, and perseverance, but these are necessary ingredients for success in anything you do, and once you get started you will enjoy it.

As you know, lawyers go to law school for three years to learn "all the laws about everything" and to learn how to research and find "all the laws." You will have only the subject of your case to research; your research is concentrated only on the legal issues raised in your case—a case you know more about than anybody else. You will have a keen and genuine personal interest in the legal issues in your own case, which makes it easier. Under these conditions, you will become an "expert" on the laws pertinent to your case in a very short time. It is easier than you think.

There are several places where you can get the information you need to handle your case. The following are listed in order of the number of books available.

LAW-SCHOOL LIBRARY

A law school is the place where you can find just about everything available anywhere. Most law-school libraries are state supported and the libraries are open to the general public. However, be sure you don't mark any books or damage them in any way, and make sure you always follow all library rules in using the books and library.

Librarians and law students are great helpers in finding anything you want. Law students are especially anxious to demonstrate how much they know about legal research, law books, and the law. You should dress appropriately for the atmosphere in a law library; and do not make noise or distract other users of the library. If you do these things, other persons will seldom cause any trouble for you. Once you get started with your research, you can have a lot of fun.

Some large law-school libraries, usually in large metropolitan areas, charge a small fee for the use of the library. In this situation, the law library is usually crowded with lawyers, professors, students, and other users. If it is too busy, you might want to go to a public library. Most public libraries in large cities will have all the books you need.

You might want to look at several sources of law, but essentially the following sources are all you really need:

- Your statutes and court rules
- Digest of your state court decisions
- Your state court Jury Instructions
- Case Reports for your state

UNIVERSITY LIBRARY

Most university libraries have a copy of your state statutes, some have the case reports, and some have the jury instructions. These are generally public libraries, and you should have no difficulty in finding what you need. Check the index first, and the librarian second!

STATE SUPREME COURT LIBRARY

If you live close to your state capital, where the state supreme court is located, you are in luck. You can use this library, but be sure you put on your best "dignity" and manners. Actually, you do not find many supreme court judges there, since their law research clerks do most of the research.

As a general rule, it is not necessary to buy "legal books." If you get involved in a lawsuit, however, you should obtain a copy of all court rules.

Glossary

ab initio — (Latin) From the beginning; from the first act; entirely; as to all the acts done; in the inception. A party can be said to be a trespasser, an estate to be good, an agreement or deed to be void, or a marriage or act to be unlawful, ab initio.

abeyance — Suspension; something that is stopped; not going forward. In property, where there is no existing person in whom a property can vest, it is said to be in abeyance until a proper owner appears.

abrogate — To annul; to abolish; to destroy.

abscond — To go in a clandestine manner out of the jurisdiction of the courts, or to lie concealed in order to avoid their process; to run away; to withdraw or absent oneself in a private manner.

abstract of title — A condensed history of the title of land, consisting of a synopsis or summary of the material or operative portion of all the conveyances, of whatever kind or nature, that in any manner affect the land or any estate or interest in it, together with a statement of all liens, charges, or liabilities to which the land may be subject, and of which it is in any way material for purchasers to be apprised.

acceptance — In contract law, consent to an offer under terms agreed to by the offeror, thereby creating a binding contract. Also, the receiving of goods with the intention of keeping them. Agreement to terms.

accident — A fortuitous circumstance, event, or happening; an event happening without any human agency, or if happening wholly or partly through human agency, an event that under the circumstances is unusual and unexpected by the person to whom it happens; an unusual, fortuitous, unexpected, unforseen, or unlooked for event, happening, or occurrence; an unusual or unexpected result attending the operation or performance of a usual or necessary act or event.

accidental — Happening by chance, or unexpectedly; taking place not according to the usual course of things; casual; fortuitous.

acknowledgment — A public declaration or formal statement of a person executing an instrument made to the official authorized to take it, that the execution of the first instrument was his free act and deed. The written evidence of an acknowledgment, which states in substance that the person named therein was known to and appeared before the official and acknowledged the instrument to be his act and deed. Generally, substantial compliance with the form or requirements laid down in the state statute is essential to the validity of a certificate of acknowledgment. An acknowledgment to an instrument generally has one of three functions: to give validity to the instrument, to permit the instrument to be introduced in evidence without other proof if execution, or to entitle the instrument to be recorded.

Act of God — An act occasioned exclusively by violence of nature without the interference of any human agency; a natural necessity proceeding from physical causes alone without the intervention of man; an act, event, happening, or occurrence; a natural and inevitable necessity implies entire exclusion of all human agency, operates without interference or aid from man, results from natural causes, and is in no sense attributable to human agency.

ad infinitum — (Latin) Without limit; to an infinite extent; indefinitely.

administration of estates — Supervision by an executor or administrator; management of an estate by an independent executor. Normally involves the collection, management, and distribution of an estate, including the legal proceedings necessary to satisfy claims of creditors, next of kin, legatees, or other parties who have any claim to the property of a deceased person.

administrator/administratrix — In probate practice, a person to whom letters of administration — that is, an authority to administer the estate of a deceased person — have been granted by the proper court. An administrator resembles an executor, but, because he is appointed by the court and not by the deceased he must give security for the due administration of the estate, by entering into a bond with sureties, called an *administration bond*.

adultery — Voluntary sexual intercourse of a married person with a person other than his or her spouse.

affidavits — A written *exparte* statement made voluntarily and sworn to or affirmed before a person legally authorized to administer an oath or affirmation. As a general rule, anyone who has knowledge of the facts sworn to in a writing may make an affidavit. Statutes or the various states prescribe the formal requisites for affidavits. Most of the statutes are quite similar, and generally prescribe the requisites as: the identification of the place where the affidavit was taken, the signature of the affiant, and the *jurat*, or certificate evidencing the fact that the affidavit has been properly made before a duly authorized officer, which properly includes the authentication.

aforethought — In criminal law, deliberate; planned; premeditated. As used in the law of murder, thought of beforehand and for any length of time, however short, before the doing of the act, and synonymous with premeditation.

agent — One who, by the authority of a principal, undertakes to transact some business or manage some affairs on account of the principal, and to render an account of it. A substitute, or deputy, appointed by his principal primarily to bring about business relations between the principal and third parties.

agency — In its broadest sense, every relation in which one person acts for or represents another by his authority. In the more restricted sense, the fiduciary relation resulting from the manifestation of consent by a principal and an agent that the agent shall act for the principal. A relation created by an agreement between the parties; a relationship between a principal and his agent; the representation of one by another the authorization of in dealing with third parties; the relation resulting from one person to another to act for him in business dealings with others.

agreement — The union of two or more minds in a thing done or to be done; a mutual assent to do a thing. A writing or instrument that is evidence of an agreement.

ambiguity — Doubtfulness; doubleness of meaning; duplicity, indistinctness, or uncertainty of meaning of an expression used in a written instrument or other document; a want of clearness or definiteness.

annulment — The act of annulling; the act of making void retrospectively as well as prospectively.

annulment of marriage — A proceeding for the purpose of declaring judicially that, because of some disability or defect that existed at the time of the marriage ceremony, no valid marriage ever took place between the parties, or that no valid marriage relation ever existed between the parties.

antenuptial — Made or done before a marriage.

antenuptial agreement — A contract made before marriage; an agreement in contemplation of marriage, usually to specify property interests of the marital partners.

appellant — The party appealing a decision or judgment to a higher court.

arraignment — In criminal practice, to bring a prisoner to the bar of the court to answer to a criminal charge.

arrest — To deprive a person of his liberty by legal authority. To take, under real or assumed authority, custody of another for the purpose of holding or detaining him to answer a criminal charge or civil demand.

arrest warrant — A written order, issued and signed by a magistrate, directing a peace officer or some other person specially named to arrest a person named in it, who is accused of an offense.

articles of incorporation — An instrument by which a private corporation is formed and organized under the general corporation laws.

articles of partnership — A written agreement by which various parties enter into a copartnership upon the terms and conditions stipulated.

assault — An intentional, unlawful offer of corporal injury to another by force, or force unlawfully directed toward the person of another, under such circumstances as to create a well-founded fear of imminent peril, coupled with apparent present ability to execute the attempt, if not prevented.

attractive nuisance doctrine — The doctrine that one who, maintains on his premises a condition — instrumental, machine, or other agency — that is dangerous to young children because of their inability to appreciate peril and that might reasonably be expected to attract them to the premises, owes a duty to exercise reasonable care to protect them against the dangers of such attraction.

battery — Any unlawful beating or other wrongful physical violence or constraint inflicted on a human being without his consent. A willful and unlawful use of force or violence upon the person of another.

bequeath — To give personal property by will to another.

bigamy — The criminal offense of willfully and knowingly contracting a second marriage, or going through a form of a second marriage, while the first marriage, to the knowledge of the offender, is still undissolved.

blue laws — Laws that prohibit the doing of certain acts on Sunday and impose sanctions for the violation of them. Commonly called Sunday statutes, Sunday closing laws, or Lord's Day Acts. At common law, with the exception of certain judicial acts, anything may be done on Sunday that may lawfully be performed on any other day of the week. In most states, regulations for observance of Sundays and holidays with corresponding sanctions for their violation have been enacted.

blue sky laws — A popular name for acts providing for the regulation and supervision of investment companies, for the protection of the community from investing in fraudulent companies. Laws intended to stop the sale of stock in fly-by-night concerns, visionary oil wells, distant gold mines, and other like fraudulent exploitations.

breach of contract — Failure, without legal excuse, to perform any promise that forms the whole or part of a contract.

breach of peace — A violation or disturbance of the public tranquility and order; the offense of breaking or disturbing the public peace by any riotous, forcible, or unlawful proceeding.

breach of warranty — A violation of an agreement as to condition, content, or quality of a good sale, not involving fraudulent misrepresentation.

bunco game — Any trick, artifice, or cunning calculated to win confidence and to deceive, whether by conversation, conduct, or suggestion.

bylaws — A rule or law of a corporation for its government, which prescribes the rights and duties of the members with reference to the internal government of the corporation, the management of its affairs, and the rights and duties existing between the members.

caveat emptor — (Latin) Literally, let the buyer beware, or take care. This maxim summarizes the rule that a purchaser must examine, judge, and test for himself. This common-law rule has been greatly restricted and modified in modern usage by many of the Consumer Protection Acts, the implied warranty of habitability in landlord-tenant relationships, the general laws of implied warranty of merchantability, and many other current laws, both federal and state, designed to protect the general public.

circumstantial evidence — All evidence of indirect nature; the process of decision by which a court or jury may reason from circumstances known or proved in order to establish by inference the principal fact.

close corporation — A corporation in which the majority of the stock is held by the officers and directors, for example, a corporation owned and operated primariy by a single family.

closed shop — A shop or business establishment having, as a condition of employment, the requirement that a person be a union member.

cohabiting — Dwelling together; living, abiding, or residing together as man and wife.

common law — Those principles, usages, and rules of action applicable to the government and security of persons and property that do not rest for their authority upon any express or positive statute or other written declaration, but upon statements of principles found in the decisions of the courts. It embraces that great body of unwritten law founded upon general custom, usage, or common consent, and based upon natural justice or reason. Historically, that body of law and juristic theory that was originated, developed and formulated in England.

common-law marriage — One not solemnized in the ordinary way, but created by an agreement to marry, between persons legally capable of making marriage contracts, followed by cohabitation. Generally, there must be a public and continued recognition of such relation by the parties, as distinguished from occasional or incidental recognition.

community property — The property acquired by either spouse during marriage, other than by gift, devise, or descent, based on the doctrine that property acquired during marriage belongs to the marital community. Community property states are Arizona, California, Idaho, Louisiana, Nevada, New Mexico, Texas, and Washington.

comparative negligence — That doctrine in the law of negligence by which the negligence of the parties is compared, and a recovery permitted, notwithstanding the contributory negligence of the plaintiff. Enacted in most states, the statute usually provides that, where the negligence of both parties is concurrent and contributes to injury, recovery of damages is not barred to plaintiff, provided that his fault is less than defendant's, and that, by the exercise of ordinary care, he could not have avoided the consequences of the defendant's negligence after it was or should have been apparent.

competency — In the law of evidence, the presence of those characteristics, or the absence of those disabilities, that render a witness legally fit and qualified to give testimony in a court of justice; applied in the same sense to documents, other written evidence, or exhibits.

compos mentis — (Latin) Sound of mind; having use and control of one's mental faculties.

condemnation — The legal process by which real estate of a private owner is taken for public use without his consent, but upon the award and payment of just compensation.

consignment — The act or process of consigning goods; the consigning of goods or cargo, especially to an agent for sale or custody; goods sent to a retailer, who is expected to pay following sale.

contempt of court — Any act that is calculated to embarrass, hinder, or obstruct a court in the administration of justice, or that is calculated to lessen its authority or its dignity. Usually

committed by a person who does any act in willful contra-
vention of its authority or dignity, or tending to impede or
frustrate the administration of justice, or by one who, being
under the court's authority as a party to a proceeding, willfully disobeys its lawful orders or fails to comply with an
undertaking which he has given.

contract—A promise, or set of promises, for the breach of
which the law gives a remedy, or for the performance of
which the law in some way recognizes a duty. An oral, written, or implied agreement between two or more persons; a
formal convenant of undertaking; an enforceable pact. Essential elements of a contract are:

1. a valid offer
2. an acceptance of the offer
3. valid consideration
4. legal capacity of the respective parties
5. legal subject matter
6. a writing, if required by law (Statute of Frauds)

corporation—An artificial person or legal entity created by or
under the authority of the laws of a state or nation, composed, in some instances, of a single person and his successors, or another corporation, being the incumbents of a particular office, but ordinarily consisting of an association of
individuals who subsist as a body politic under a special
denomination. Regarded in law as having a personality and
existence distinct from that of its members, and, by the same
authority, vested with the capacity of continuous succession, irrespective of changes in the membership, either in
perpetuity or for a limited term of years, and of acting as a
unit or single individual in matters relating to the common
purpose of the association, within the scope of the powers
and authorities conferred upon such bodies by law.

corpus delicti—(Latin) The body of a crime; the body (material
substance) upon which a crime has been committed, for
example, the corpse of a murdered man, the charred remains of a house burned down, or other evidence. In a
derivative sense, the substance or foundation of a crime the
substantial fact that a crime has been committed.

crime—An offense against the state or sovereignty; an act
committed, or omitted, in violation of a public law forbidding, or commanding, it. A wrong that the government

claims is injurious to the public at large and punishes through a judicial proceeding in the name of the state. An act in violation of a statute declaring it unlawful, but prescribing no penalty, does not constitute a crime. For example, in some states fornication and adultery are prohibited, but carry no fines or penalties; seldom are they prosecuted or convictions obtained.

descent — Transmission of an estate by inheritance, usually to a descendant.

devise — A giving or disposing of real property by will; a will or clause of a will that performs this function.

disposing memory — A memory in which a person can recall the general nature, condition, and extent of property and his relations to those to whom he gives and to those from whom he withholds that property.

divorce — The legal separation of a man and wife, effected for cause by the judgment of a court, and either totally dissolving the marriage relation, or suspending its effects so far as concerns the cohabitation of the parties. Many states have now enacted no-fault statutes, in which the term *dissolution of marriage* is used.

doing business — Within statutes on service of process on foreign corporations, conducting or managing business. The exercise in a state of some of the ordinary functions for which a corporation foreign to that state was organized. A foreign corporation is amenable to process within a state if it does business in the state in such a manner as to warrant the inference that it is present there or that it has subjected itself to the jurisdiction and laws in which the service is made. What constitutes doing business depends on the facts in each particular case, and the wording of the statute.

domestic corporation — A corporation that is incorporated under the laws of a state, as opposed to a foreign corporation, which is incorporated under the laws of another state or nation.

domicile — A place of true, fixed, and permanent home and principal establishment, to which a person, whenever he is absent, has the intention of returning. The legal concept of home.

double indemnity — A clause in a life or accident insurance policy that grants double payment of the policy's face amount if death results from accident.

Dram Shop Act — A civil damage statute directed at the operations of dram shops and at owners of buildings and premises in which the operators are tenants, and permitting an action to be brought by a person who has been injured by an intoxicated person against one who contributed to the intoxication.

et al — (Latin) Abbreviation for *et alii,* and others.

et seq. — (Latin) Abbreviation for *et sequentes* or *et sequentia,* and the following.

fee simple estate — An estate in which the owner is entitled to the entire property, with unconditional power of disposition during his life, and descending to his heirs and legal representatives upon his death intestate. The word *fee,* used alone, is a sufficient designation of this species of estate, and hence *simple* is not a necessary part of the title, but it is added as a means of distinguishing this estate from any variety of conditional estates. Also called *absolute estate.*

forcible detainer — A detainer used in cases where one originally in rightful possession of realty refuses to surrender it at the termination of his possessory right.

forcible entry — A violent taking of lands and tenements with force and arms, against the will of those entitled to the possession, and without the authority of law. Accompanied with circumstances tending to excite terror in the occupant, and to prevent him from maintaining his rights. Angry words and threats of force may be sufficient.

forcible entry and detainer — A summary court proceeding for restoring the possession of land to one who is wrongfully kept out or has been wrongfully deprived of the possession.

foreign corporation — A corporation created by or under the authority of the laws of another state, government, or country.

fornication — Unlawful sexual intercourse between two unmarried persons. If one person is married and the second is not, it is fornication on the part of the second person, but adultery for the first. By statute in some states, however, it is adultery on the part of both persons if the woman is married, whether the man is married or not.

fortuitous — Happening by chance or accident; occurring unexpectedly or without known cause; accidental, undesigned, adventitious; resulting from unavoidable physical causes.

franchising — A form of marketing and distribution in which a parent company is termed the *franchisor;* the purchaser of the privilege, the *franchisee;* and the right, or privilege itself, a *franchise.* The privilege may be quite varied. It may be the right to sell the parent company's products, to use his name, to adopt his methods, or to copy his symbols, trademarks, or architecture; or the franchise may include all of these rights. The time period and the size of the area of business operations, which are specified, also may vary greatly.

fraud — An intentional perversion of truth for the purpose of inducing another in reliance upon it to part with some valuable thing belonging to him or to surrender a legal right. A false representation of a matter of fact, whether by words or by conduct, by false or misleading allegations, or by concealment of that which should have been disclosed, which deceives and is intended to deceive another so that he acts upon it to his legal injury. Any kind of artifice employed by one person to deceive another. Synonyms: bad faith, cheat, chicanery, deceit, dishonesty, duplicity, faithlessness, infidelity, machinations, perfidy, swindle, unfairness.

fraudulent representation — A false statement as to a material fact, made with the intent that another rely thereon, which is believed by the other party and on which he relies and by which he is induced to act and does act to his injury. A statement is fraudulent if the speaker knows the statement to be false or if it is made with utter disregard of its truth or falsity.

gift causa mortis — A gift of personalty made in expectation of death, then imminent, or an essential condition that the property shall belong fully to the donee in case the donor dies as anticipated, leaving the donee surviving him, and the gift is not in the meantime revoked.

gift inter vivos — A gift between the living, which is perfected and becomes absolute during the lifetime of the donor and the donee.

habeas corpus — (Latin) Literally, you have the body. The name given a variety of writs whose object it is to bring a person before a court or judge. In common usage, it is directed to the official or person detaining another, commanding him to produce the body of the prisoner or person detained so the court can determine if such person has been denied his liberty without due process of law.

holographic will — A testamentary instrument entirely written, dated, and signed by the testator in his own handwriting. In some states, by statute, based on the Uniform Probate Code, it is only required that the signature and the material provisions of the will be in the testator's handwriting.

illegal — Not authorized by law; illicit; unlawful; contrary to law.

illegality — That which is contrary to the principles of law, as distinguished from mere rules of procedure. It denotes a complete defect in the proceedings.

illicit — Not permitted or allowed; prohibited; unlawful; as an illicit trade or act.

incompetency — Lack of ability, legal qualification, or fitness to discharge the required duty.

insanity — Unsoundness of mind; madness; mental alienation or derangement; a morbid psychiatric condition resulting from disorder of the brain, whether arising from malformation or defective organization or morbid processes affecting the brain primarily or diseased states of general system implicating it secondarily, which involves the intellect, the emotions, the will, and the moral sense, or some of these faculties, and which is characterized especially by their non-development, derangement, or perversion, and is manifested, in most forms, by delusions, incapacity to reason or to judge, or uncontrollable impulses. In law, such a want of reason, memory, and intelligence as prevents a man from comprehending the nature and consequences of his acts or from distinguishing between right and wrong conduct. Insanity does not generally include certain states of transitory mental disorders, as trances, epilepsy, hysteria, and delirium.

insolvency — The condition of a person who is insolvent; an inability to pay one's debts; having a lack of means to pay one's debts. One who is unable to pay debts as they fall due, or in the usual course of trade or business.

intent — Design, resolve, or determination with which a person acts. Intent, being a state of mind, is rarely susceptible of direct proof, but must ordinarily be inferred from the facts. Intent presupposes knowledge. In the legal sense, a purpose to use a particular means to effect certain results. Compare *motive*.

inter vivos — (Latin) Between the living; from one living person to another; pertaining to gifts given during one's lifetime.

intestate — Having made no will; dying, without leaving anything to testify what one's wishes were with respect to the disposal of one's property after one's death.

intestate succession — A succession occurring when the deceased has left no will, or when his will has been revoked or annulled as irregular. The heirs to whom a succession has fallen by the effects of law only are called heirs *ab intestato*.

ipso facto — (Latin) By the fact itself; by the mere fact; by the mere effect of an act or a fact.

joint tenancy — Common ownership of property by two or more persons, with the property passing to the surviving person or persons at the death of one co-owner.

John Doe — A fictitious name frequently used to indicate a person for the purpose of argument or illustration, or in the course of enforcing a fiction in the law. The name that was usually given to the fictitious lessee of the plaintiff in the mixed action of ejectment. The name is, and for some centuries has been, used in legal proceedings to designate a party until his real name can be ascertained.

jurisdiction — A term of large and comprehensive import, embracing every kind of judicial action. The authority by which courts and judicial officers take cognizance of and decide cases; the legal right by which judges exercise their authority. It exists when a court has cognizance of the class of cases involved, proper parties are present, and the point to be decided is within the issues presented.

larceny — Felonious stealing, taking and carrying, leading, riding, or driving away another's personalty with an intent to convert it or to deprive the owner of it.

libel — In tort law, defamation expressed by print, writing, pictures, or signs; any publication that is injurious to the reputation of another; defamatory words read aloud by speaker from written articles and broadcast by radio. An accusation in writing or printing against the character of a person which affects his reputation, in that it tends to hold him up to hatred, abuse, ridicule, contempt, shame, disgrace, or obloquy, to degrade him in the estimation of the community, to induce an evil opinion of him in the minds of other persons, to make him an object of reproach, to diminish his respectability or abridge his comforts, to change his position in society for the worse, to dishonor or discredit him in the estimation of the public, or his friends and acquaintances, or to deprive him of friendly intercourse in society, or cause him to be shunned or avoided, or where it is charged that one has violated his public duty as a public officer.

libelous per se — Pertaining to words of such a character that an action may be brought upon them without the necessity of showing any special damage, the imputation being that the law will presume anyone so slandered must have suffered damage.

limited partnership — A partnership in which the liability of some members, but not all, is limited; such a partnership may be formed under most state statutes, which permit an individual to contribute a specific sum of money to the capital of the partnership and limit his liability for losses to that amount, upon the partnership complying with the requirements of the statutes.

long-arm statute — A statute allowing a court to obtain jurisdiction over a defendant located outside the normal jurisdiction of the court.

motive — Reason that leads a mind to desire a certain result. Compare *intent*.

Negligence — Failure to do something that a reasonable person, guided by those ordinary considerations which ordinarily regulate human affairs, would do, or committing an act that a reasonable and prudent person would not do.

obscene—As defined by some statutes, that which, considered as a whole, predominately appeals to prurient interest; that is, a lustful or morbid interest in nudity, sex, sexual conduct, sexual excitement, excretion, sadism, masochism, or sadomasochistic abuse, which goes substantially beyond customary limits of candor in describing, portraying, or dealing with such ;matters, and which is utterly without redeeming social value.

partnership—A voluntary contract between two or more competent persons to place their money, effects, labor, and skill, or some or all of them, in lawful commerce or business, with the understanding that there shall be proportional sharing of the profits and losses between them. An association of two or more persons to carry on as co-owners a business for profit.

per capital—Equally, or share and share alike.

per stirpes—According to the roots, or by right of representation. The issue of deceased children will take their deceased parent's share by right of representation. That mode of reckoning the rights or liabilities of descendants in which the children of any one descendant take only the share that their parent would have taken, if alive.

perjury—The willful assertion as a matter of fact, opinion, belief, or knowledge made by a witness in a judicial proceeding as a part of his evidence, either upon oath or in any form allowed by law to be substituted for an oath, whether such evidence is given in open court, or in an affidavit, or otherwise, such assertion being material to the issue or point of inquiry and known to such witness to be false.

piercing the corporate veil—In cases involving fraud or unjust enrichment, the courts refusal to recognize a corporation as an entity separate from those responsible for corporate activity, and holding the corporation's alter ego liable.

power of attorney—An insturemnt authorizing another to act as one's agent or attorney-in-fact.

prima facie—(Latin) At first sight; on the first appearance; on the face of it; so far as can be judged from the first disclosure, presumably; pertaining to a fact presumed to be true unless disproved by some evidence to the contrary.

pro se—For himself; on his own behalf; in person. Usually used to designate a person who represents himself in a court case.

probate — The presenting of a will to the appropriate court to establish its validity, and the entering of the court's order finding that the instrument is decedent's will and admitting it to "probate."

proximate cause — That which, in the natural and continuous sequence, unbroken by an efficient intervening cause, produces the injury, and without which the result would not have occurred.

prurient — (Latin, *pruriens* or *prurire*, to itch or long for a thing, to be lecherous.) Inclined or inclining to lascivious thoughts; bringing about lasciviousness or lust; eagerly desirous.

reasonable — Just; proper; ordinary or usual; fit and appropriate to the end in view, having the faculty of reason; agreeable to reason.

reasonable doubt — That state of the minds of jurors in which they cannot say they feel an abiding conviction as to the truth of a charge.

relevant — Applying to the matter in question; affording something to the purpose.

res ipsa loquitur — (Latin) Literally, the thing speaks for itself. Rebuttable presumption that defendant was negligent, which arises upon proof that instrumentality causing injury was in the defendant's exclusive control, and that the accident was one which ordinarily does not happen in the absence of negligence.

rescission of contract — An annulling or abrogation or unmaking of a contract and the placing of the parties to it in status quo.

residuary clause — A clause in a will by which that part of the property is disposed of which remains after satisfying bequests and devises.

revocation of will — The recalling, annulling, or rendering inoperative an existing will, by some subsequent act of the testator, which might be by the making of a new will inconsistent with the terms of the first, or the destruction of the old will, or the disposal of the property to which it related, or otherwise.

slander — The speaking of base and defamatory words tending to prejudice another in his reputation, office, trade, business, or means of livelihood.

Statute of Frauds — The common designation of a very celebrated English statute passed in 1677, which has been adopted in a more or less modified form in all states in this country. Its chief characteristic is the provision that no suit or action shall be maintained on certain classes of contracts or engagements unless there is note or memorandum thereof in writing signed by the party to be charged or by his authorized agent. Its object was to close the door to the numerous frauds and perjuries.

subpoena — A process to cause a witness to appear and give testimony, commanding him to lay aside all pretenses and excuses, and appear before a court or magistrate therein named at a time therein mentioned to testify for the party named under a penalty therein mentioned.

summons — A writ, directed to the sheriff or other proper officer, requiring him to notify the person named that an action has been commenced against him in the court whence the writ issues, and that he is required to appear, on a day named, and answer the complaint in such action.

tenant — One who holds or possesses lands or tenements by any kind of right or title, whether in fee, for life, for years, at will, or otherwise.

testamentary — The expression of an intent to dispose of property in a will.

testator — One who dies leaving a will.

tort — A legal concept possessing the basic element of a wrong with resultant injury and consequential damage which is cognizable in a court of law. That great body of law described generally as a civil wrong — assault and battery, personal injury from auto accidents, libel and slander, malicious prosecution, and other personal types of hurt. The three elements of every tort action are: existence of a legal duty from the defendant to the plaintiff, breach of that duty, and damage as a proximate result.

trademark — A distinctive mark, motto, device, or emblem that a manufacturer stamps, prints, or otherwise affixes to the goods he produces, so that they can be identified in the market and their origin vouched for.

trade name — A name that is used in trade to designate a particular business of certain individuals considered somewhat as an entity, or the place at which a business is located, or a class of goods, but that is not a technical trademark either because it is not applied or affixed to goods sent into the market or because it is not capable of exclusive appropriation by anyone as a trademark. Trade names may, or may not, be exclusive.

trespass — To commit an unlawful act or a lawful act in unlawful manner in injury of another's person or property.

trust — In general, a right of property, real or personal, held by one party for the benefit of another.

trustee — One to whom property or funds have been legally entrusted to be administered for the benefit of another; a person, usually one of the persons appointed to administer the affairs of a company, institution, or the like.

trustor — One who creates a trust. Also called a *settlor.*

unconscionable bargain — A bargain or contract in which no man in his senses, not under delusion, would make, on the one hand, and which no fair and honest man would accept, on the other.

unconscionable conduct — Conduct that is monstrously harsh and shocking to the conscience.

void — Having no legal or binding force; null; empty or not containing matter; vacant; unoccupied; devoid; destitute.

warranty — In general, a promise that the goods are reasonably fit for the general purpose for which they are sold.

will — An instrument executed by a competent person in the manner prescribed by statute, whereby he makes a disposition of his property to take effect on and after his death.

Index

Index

226

Other Bestsellers From TAB

Other Bestsellers From TAB